LEADING
COMPLEX
PROJECTS

LEADING COMPLEX PROJECTS

A Data-Driven Approach to Mastering the Human Side of Project Management

Edward W. Merrow and
Neeraj S. Nandurdikar

WILEY

Library of Congress Cataloging-in-Publication Data

Names: Merrow, Edward W., author. | Nandurdikar, Neeraj S., author.
Title: Leading complex projects : a data-driven approach to mastering the human side of project management / by Edward W. Merrow and Neeraj S. Nandurdikar.
Description: Hoboken, New Jersey : John Wiley & Sons, Inc., [2018] | Includes index. |
Identifiers: LCCN 2018008707 (print) | ISBN 9781119382195 (cloth)
Subjects: LCSH: Project management.
Classification: LCC HD69.P75 M474 2018 (print) | DDC 658.4/04--dc23
LC record available at https://lccn.loc.gov/2018008707

ISBN 978-1-119-38219-5 (hbk)
ISBN 978-1-119-38225-6 (ebk)
ISBN 978-1-119-38226-3 (ebk)

10 9 8 7 6 5 4 3 2 1

This book is dedicated to families.

First, the families of the authors who put up with the constant stress of our travel and yet happily encouraged us to write this book.

Second, our IPA family — everyone at IPA who made our work possible by doing the difficult and exacting work of collecting data on thousands of projects and turning those data into useable information.

And third, to the family of project directors — the project management family — that we have come to know and embrace over the last several decades and from whom we continue to learn every day.

CONTENTS

FOREWORD

All companies, governments, and even individuals desire to have their projects completed with success. In the industrial world, this elusive success has always been measured in terms of performance against project goals, normally quantified in terms of safety, quality, cost, and schedule. To be successful in today's regulatory and commercial environment requires that we deliver exceptional performance on all four of these measures. Many methods are available to track the goals and achievements of the desired performance. Yet, even with numerous methods, processes, and procedures, major projects continue to have significant failure rates (discussed in significant detail in *Industrial Megaprojects* by Ed Merrow). This new book provides additional insight into major project execution that looks beyond the usual processes and recognizes the critical factor: project success *is all about people.* Therefore, the true differentiator for project performance is the *leadership of the people* developing and executing the project.

With all the literature available on leadership, why should you spend your time with this specific book? I believe that the authors have captured the essence of creating successful projects with their analysis of leadership as it applies specifically to large industrial projects. This analysis builds upon the library of recognized experts such as Bennis, Goleman, and others. Using the proprietary database of Independent Project Analysis, Inc., which includes thousands of projects covering many industries, Ed and Neeraj have studied specific, successful projects. Through surveys and direct interviews, they have determined what each project leader did that helped his or her team to succeed. I think you will find valuable guidance in this book for the selection of the leader for your next major capital project, as well as keys to building an excellent project management organization. This can provide a basis for future success through investment in the people in your organization.

In the interview section of the book, the authors share insights from several successful project leaders. The varied backgrounds, industries, experiences, ways of handling teams and significant issues will provide valuable comparisons for your consideration. A consistent thread is the focus on teams and relationships to enable project success. These relationships include the supply chain for projects, including vendors and contractors, assuring an integrated process. In this book you will see the importance of *values* in driving project success. You will see how the personal values of the leaders create a shared culture in the project that governs how people communicate and trust each other to assure best-for-project decisions and keep projects moving toward success. Where the company culture aligns with the project culture, significant empowerment of the team provides an additional enabler of success. And where the right company culture doesn't exist, these leaders still often find ingenious ways to work around that and create inspiration and followership and still deliver success. That's what leadership is about!

I encourage you to read on and enjoy this fresh approach to understanding this driver of major capital project success.

Don Vardeman
Vice President of Worldwide
Project Management (Retired)
Anadarko Petroleum Corporation

Acknowledgments

Just like any other project, the making of this book was a collaboration among a great many people, many of whom donated their time because of their belief in the importance of effective project leadership. First, we thank the 56 leaders of complex projects who completed our detailed survey as well as the complex projects that went with them. Without their help this would have been quite impossible. Second, we thank the seven extraordinary project leaders who were willing to sit for long interviews with us to deepen our understanding of how successful project leaders approach their important work. These seven are the real authors of Part II of this book.

We also owe a deep debt to those researchers whose life's work was essential to our analysis, particularly Lewis Goldberg, developer of the Five-Factor Model version that we employed, and Daniel Goleman, a central developer of the connections between emotional intelligence and effective leadership.

We also thank our external reviewers: Joseph C. Brewer, Jr., Paul Harris, Robert Don Vardeman, Murray Covello, and William Hederman. These gentlemen provided a practitioner's reading that enriched the effort. We would like to thank Jon Walker of IPA's research organization, who both pioneered some of the methodology we employ and was also kind enough to review some of the key chapters of the book. We also thank Lucas Milrod, deputy director of IPA Projects Research Division/Organization and Teams, who both reviewed chapters and provided answers to many questions about psychological research as we proceeded. Our thanks to Elizabeth Sanborn and Loretta Merrow, who reviewed some of the early chapters. We also thank Katya Petrochenkov, a senior research analyst in our UK office, who read and commented on the draft. We were helped throughout by Kelli Ratliff's eye for graphics, which she combines with knowing the substance, an unbeatable combination. Thanks also to our Wiley editor, Richard Narramore, and our Wiley team.

Finally, and most especially, we would like to thank our spouses, Loretta and Christine, who put up with our additional stress as we wrote this book while trying to do our day jobs.

About the Authors

Edward W. Merrow is the founder and CEO of Independent Project Analysis, Inc. After starting his career as a professor at the University of California, Los Angeles, Ed spent 15 years at the RAND Corporation, eventually directing RAND's Energy Research Program. In 1987 he founded IPA to be a unique benchmarking and research provider to the capital-intensive industries and infrastructure builders around the world. Ed has authored a number of studies and books, most recently *Industrial Megaprojects* (Wiley, 2011). Ed's contributions to the industry have been recognized by a number of organizations and he is a member of the National Academy of Construction.

Neeraj S. Nandurdikar is Director of IPA's global Exploration and Production (E&P) practice. In this capacity he acts as a partner and adviser to Fortune 100 Oil and Gas executives around the world in helping to find savings and efficiencies across the entire oil and gas value chain and lift capital productivity. He has delivered several keynotes and conference presentations and is a key thought leader in the industry, working to enhance the oil and gas industry's capital projects performance and make the industry stronger and more resilient. He has an MBA from the Wharton Business School of University of Pennsylvania and an MS in Petroleum Engineering from the University of Tulsa.

EXECUTIVE SUMMARY

There is general agreement throughout the industrial world that large complex projects have had a very rough go. There have been a number of books and articles published seeking to diagnose why the track record has been so bleak and even (somewhat naïve) calls to stop doing megaprojects altogether in the future.[1] The problems are not new and have been documented by academics, the trade press, and occasionally even the daily news for at least 30 years.[2] Nor are the problems confined to any particular sector. Flyvbjerg et al. document the problems in public infrastructure projects.[3] Merrow (2011) has reported the record of the petroleum, chemicals, and minerals industries.[4] It's not a pretty picture. Megaprojects fail more than twice as often as their under-$1 billion counterparts using the same criteria for failure.

---

[1] Tim Haidar and Clare Colhoun, "Death of the Megaprojects?" *Oil and Gas IQ*, January 2018.

[2] Peter Morris and George Hough, *The Anatomy of Major Projects: A Study of the Reality of Project Management* (Wiley, 1987); Edward Merrow, *A Quantitative Analysis of Very Large Civilian Projects* (The Rand Corporation, 1988); Edward Merrow and Ralph Shangraw, "Understanding the Costs of Schedules of World Bank Supported Hydroelectric Projects," Energy Series Paper No. 31 (Washington, DC: The World Bank, 1990); "Road to Tragedy: A History of Big Dig Problems" and "Comparing the Big Dig's Costs to Megaprojects Around the World," *Boston Globe*, December 29, 2015.

[3] Bent Flyvbjerg, Nils Bruzelius, and Werner Rothengatter, *Megaprojects and Risk: An Anatomy of Ambition* (Cambridge University Press, 2002).

[4] Edward Merrow, *Industrial Megaprojects* (Hoboken, NJ: Wiley, 2011).

Amidst all this discussion of failure it is easy to overlook the fact that about one complex project in three is highly successful. The successes are too numerous to be dismissed as flukes. In *Industrial Megaprojects* (2011) we showed that when large complex projects followed a particular set of practices, they were quite likely to generate not just good but genuinely excellent outcomes. This indicated that success and failure were not in any sense random. What we could not satisfactorily explain is why relatively so few megaprojects actually employed sound practices. The failure to do so could not be explained by ignorance because the practices are known throughout the modern projects world, especially over the past 15 years. We rationalized some of the failure away by noting how difficult getting the right work done is for complex projects. But that still failed to explain why the successes were able to accomplish in practices what the failures could not.

The missing piece of the puzzle is to be found in the nature of project leadership, how leaders are selected for complex projects, and how they must behave to achieve success. Although we noted in *Industrial Megaprojects* that leaders have a disproportionate effect on project results in complex projects, we did not deeply investigate why. That is the subject of this book.

We considered titling this book *The Leadership of Megaprojects*. But that title would have obscured an essential point: the characteristic that generates so many problems for megaprojects is that most of them are complex, and it is complexity rather than size that triggers the pathway to failure. When smaller projects have the same degree of complexity, they too have an equally high rate of disappointing projects. They are simply much less likely to be complex.

Complexity occurs in three dimensions in projects: scope, organization, and shaping. *Scope complexity* occurs when a project has a number of distinct elements, drawing on different technical disciplines, all of which must be fully and carefully coordinated to produce a valuable result. Scope complexity is exacerbated by uncertainty in the basic technical data underpinning designs in many large projects. Petroleum development projects, for example, always have a major basic data development challenge in trying to understand the reservoir being developed. Scope complexity is the most common source of *organizational complexity*. The project organization is complex when a number of separate teams are required to execute the scope. These teams are often required because the technical disciplines needed to develop the area of work are distinct. Organizational complexity is also created in project systems that organize by function rather than by project teams led by an authoritative director. Finally, shaping is the process by which the benefits of a project are allocated among the various stakeholders along with the allocation of costs and management of risks. *Shaping complexity* is high when the stakeholder set that must be aligned around the project is diverse and potentially quarrelsome, usually with both private and public-sector players.

There are all sorts of reasons that complexity makes projects more difficult, but the biggest problem that complexity presents is that complexity transforms the leadership requirements for a project from the arena of project management to the realm of project leadership. In a complex project, the person at the top cannot watch the performance of most of those involved. In a complex project, the leader cannot demand compliance from recalcitrant stakeholders. Leadership is the art of getting full cooperation from those who are not forced to comply. Unfortunately, those responsible for selecting project directors for complex projects are usually not aware of the transformed requirements.

Figure I.1
The Leadership of Complex Projects

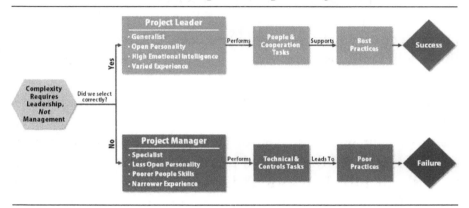

Good project managers are good organizers. They plan out the tasks that need to be accomplished and the order in which those tasks are to be done. They then assign tasks to those with the disciplinary competence to execute them and hold everyone accountable for delivering their part of the work on time and budget. Good project managers can be quite transactional about the whole process and be quite successful.

Complexity requires leaders at the top of the project rather than project managers. Some project managers are by nature and development both leaders and managers, but most are not. When the wrong selection process is used and the wrong person is selected to sit atop a complex project, failure regularly follows. The whole process is illustrated in Figure I.1.

PROJECT LEADERS VERSUS PROJECT MANAGERS

In our study of the directors of complex projects, we find that successful leaders display very different personalities and backgrounds from the unsuccessful leaders, but the unsuccessful leaders look very much like the profiles of most project managers of simpler projects. The usual selection process for new complex project leaders is to draw from the pool of successful project managers of simple projects. Sometimes they have the "right stuff," as Tom Wolfe would say, and sometimes they don't.

To investigate what constitutes the right stuff we administered a battery of psychological tests to 56 complex project leaders along with a survey of their backgrounds and career development. We then linked this information statistically to the tasks that the leaders found valuable and spent their time on and finally to the practices executed on the projects. Successful project leaders have a generalist orientation, although they may have started their careers as effective technical specialists. They are unusually open personalities, and especially so when one considers that all of our sample consisted of engineers by original training. Open personalities are better learners on the whole and deal with uncertainty much more easily than those who measure as more closed. Open personalities are more likely to listen to more points of view as well. Among the seven successful leaders with whom we conducted in-depth interviews, we found that most had very clear and well-articulated approaches to learning.

The successful leaders scored higher on five of the six scales measuring different attributes of emotional intelligence.[5] Emotional intelligence is different than standard IQ. Emotional intelligence measures people skills and overall facility with recognizing and using emotions. Such skills might be a plus for the manager of a simple project, but they are a must

---

[5] On the only scale in which successful leaders were not higher — regulating emotions — the reason is that both groups were equally high. This scale measures one's ability to keep one's cool.

for project leaders because project leaders are not so much governors of tasks as they are leaders of managers and aligners of stakeholders. Strong people skills are integral to effective leadership.

Successful leaders tended to have had a more varied career, especially early on. They were more likely to have worked for another company in another industry before settling into their career. They were much more likely to have worked as a liaison in a joint venture operated by another company than unsuccessful leaders.

What Successful Leaders Do

Personality and emotional intelligence don't develop and execute projects. What they do, however, is shape the tasks that project leaders like to do and find important to do. Leaders with open personalities with high emotional intelligence focused their work on communication, people management, stakeholder management, and working with people in the supply chain. Those with more black-and-white personalities found dealing with emotions more difficult and focused their attention on work process, project management tasks, controls, and engineering tasks. In other words, those that had failed complex projects focused on the classical project management tasks. Those who succeeded focused on the classical leadership tasks. Not a very surprising conclusion but one that is rewarding to actually prove.

A successful project leader is able to get the needed practices accomplished at the right time while their failing colleagues cannot. The reader should recognize that getting the right things done at the right time for complex projects is very difficult. It requires that a lot of things are accomplished in a short period of time by people who often have never worked together before. Implementing the right practices at the right time is a manifestation of the ability of the successful complex project leader to generate extraordinary levels of cooperation from all involved.

FROM TASKS TO PRACTICES

Of course, at the end of the day, it is good practices, especially upfront, combined with dedicated people ready to react to the inevitable surprises, that actually get projects done successfully. A seeming paradox in our analysis is that those complex project leaders who focused on work process and practices rather than leadership weren't able to get the practices done correctly. Those who focused on leadership were. The resolution of the paradox is simple – the job of the leader is to facilitate others getting the practices done properly by keeping everyone focused on the goals of the project and keeping at bay all the stakeholders who might be tempted to disrupt the progress of the project. The leader's job is not only to give vision and to guide but also to protect the good work being done by others.

If your goal is to improve the results of the most important projects that you do, you must focus on how you are selecting the people who lead them. This book tells you how to do that.

CHAPTER 1
GETTING GROUNDED

There are literally thousands of books about project management and how it should be done for all manner of projects, large and small. But, ironically, there are almost no books about project managers, the people who actually organize and lead projects and get the work done. In this book we explore the makeup of a particular subset of project managers: those who lead major complex projects for the sponsors (owners) of the projects.[1] The leaders of large complex projects usually carry the title of project director rather than project manager. We will use that term or simply *project leader* to differentiate them from the managers of simpler projects or of the subprojects that usually accompany a large, complex capital venture.

Management is all about the efficient organization of tasks in a project, making rational assignments to team members and contractors based on their strengths, monitoring performance of individuals and teams, and getting work accomplished. All projects require management or they will fail. But not all projects require leadership.

---

[1] We will define and discuss complexity at some length in Chapter 3 as it bears the nature of the leader's role. Suffice it to say, complex projects are undertakings with a number of areas of scope, lots of stakeholders, both internal and external, and a degree of organizational complexity. Almost all megaprojects are complex, but many projects below the megaproject threshold of a billion dollars or so are also complex projects and must be treated accordingly to succeed.

Leadership is rather different from management even if exercised by the same person. Leadership is all about *inducing* people to cooperate in pursuing a goal (a vision if you prefer) that the leader has articulated. The notion of leadership implies followership. The notion of followership implies a degree of volition. We contend that smaller, simpler projects can usually be managed without much true leadership, but large complex projects must always be led. We understand, of course, that this is a matter of degree and situation. For example, a small project staffed entirely by volunteers may require leadership as well as management because the staff can walk away if they are unhappy or even bored. Those who sponsor and invest in projects must come to understand which projects require leaders and what characteristics of those leaders help predict which candidate will most likely be successful. Providing that knowledge is the primary goal of this book.

We have known for some time that the fate of difficult projects seems to hinge more on the project leaders than the results of simpler projects.[2] In complex projects, the loss of continuity in project leadership at any point from the start of project execution planning forward results in much worse outcomes with the failure rate more than doubling. The effect is present in simpler projects too, but the effect on outcomes is much larger in complex projects. Our goal in undertaking the research that led to this book was to understand the personalities, prior experience, and habits of mind that make some complex project leaders successful while others fail. The reason that this book is needed is that far too many large complex projects fail. We have become convinced through the course of this research that one of the major reasons why so many

---

[2] See Edward Merrow, *Industrial Megaprojects* (Hoboken, NJ: Wiley, 2011), 180–182.

complex projects fail is because the leader was miscast in his or her role.

THE SELECTION PROCESS FOR COMPLEX PROJECT LEADERS IS NOT WORKING

We conclude from the analysis described in Chapters 4 and 5 of this book that the process that industrial companies are using to select leaders for their most important projects is broken. Before we dive into what leads us to that conclusion, we describe how the current selection process actually works.

To better understand how leaders are actually selected for complex projects, we surveyed 13 industrial companies, all in the petroleum industry, that have numerous complex megaprojects in their portfolios. All of the companies will typically have multiple multibillion-dollar projects underway at any point so their need for complex project leaders is sustained. We asked representatives of the companies how project leaders are selected, by whom, and at what point in time in the project's evolution. We were fortunate to have multiple responses from most companies because the multiple responses indicated the extent to which the selection process is consistent and understood. At least one representative from each company was a senior manager within the project's organization. Forty-nine people completed the survey, giving us an average of almost four responses per company.

Who Selects the Leaders?

Eight of the 13 companies reported that complex project leaders are selected by senior management within the projects organization, although one of those eight indicated that a "functional professional development committee" within the project organization made the assignment. In three cases a senior business executive selected the project leader, and in two cases the selection is made jointly by the business and projects. While one might guess that selection by a business executive would be more common in smaller companies where the business professionals are more likely to know the project leaders personally, there is actually no pattern at all. Rather, sole selection by the business appears to reflect weakness in the project's organization. In the cases of joint selection, one company is a very large, nationally owned company and the other a much smaller independent.

What Are the Selection Criteria?

While the selection criteria are not exactly random, there is not much hint of scientific method. Experience – undefined – was the most commonly cited criterion followed by availability, and then by "politics or favoritism."[3] Of our total of 49 respondents, only two claimed that any personality characteristics were included in the selection criteria, although one indicated that language skills and cultural understanding were important. Two respondents indicated that familiarity with the technology to be used on the project was important.

The picture that emerges from our survey is of selection processes that are largely ad hoc. Experience, which we

---

[3] We must note that experience does not necessarily equate to good experience. We do have cases in which the project leader has presided over a distinctly poor complex project, only to be assigned to another thereafter. We even know of cases in which a project leader has had successive failed megaprojects with no track record of success on such projects. What this suggests, of course, is that finding people who are considered qualified to lead these difficult projects is itself quite difficult.

take to mean prior track record of success, is important but relatively little else. There are several problems with this approach. First, at any point in time, a significant fraction of all complex project leaders will be doing their first complex project. This is because most project managers who graduate to complex project leadership have already spent 20 years in project management and therefore have only one or two megaprojects left in their careers.[4] Only in the most unusual cases do we see more than two or three complex projects in a career. This means that the experience measure that companies are using is often based on performance on less complex projects. Unfortunately, there is no evidence to support the notion that successful experience on less complex projects is a good predictor of success in difficult projects. The great majority of those selected to lead their first complex projects were successful simpler-project managers. Success in one's first complex project is a good predictor of success in a second. But it is not even clear that a long career progression in smaller, less complex projects is of any substantial value to the complex project leader at all. A few of our most successful leaders were assigned – usually out of necessity – to their first complex project at an earlier (inexperienced) point in their careers. A few more of our most successful leaders had never actually managed *any* capital project prior to their first megaproject, although they had been in positions that were closely aligned with projects, such as disciplinary heads of engineering. If an effective selection process were in place to identify effective project leader candidates earlier in their careers, it would significantly increase the supply of these critical human resources.

---

[4] The average complex project requires four to five years in execution preceded by more than two years (often much more) in front-end planning and development.

When Are Project Directors Usually Installed?

There is an ongoing debate within the industrial megaprojects community about what constitutes the ideal time to appoint and install the leader for projects. The point of contention is whether leaders who are adept at developing the right scope for a project also have the right skills (and perhaps temperament) to execute a project. Those who believe that the temperaments and skillsets are necessarily different argue to bring the project leader on at the beginning of FEL 3[5] or even at the start of detailed engineering rather than earlier in front-end loading. Those who believe that a single project leader can lead the entire process want the project leader involved as early as reasonably practical so that the project leader deeply understands the scope.

We asked our survey respondents when project directors are usually appointed for their projects and in those cases in which they were installed at the start of scope development whether they actually controlled the scope development process or acted more in an observer role. The results are shown in Figure 1.1. One of the 13 companies represented in the survey brings the leader on at the beginning of FEL 1 and makes that leader accountable for scope development.[6] Six companies bring the leader onto the projects at the start of scope development and five of those six make the project leader responsible for scope development. Two companies bring the leader on after the basic scope is developed but still during the FEL 2 (scope development) phase of the project.

---

[5] FEL stands for "front-end loading," which is the process by which a project is conceptualized, developed, and defined prior to the start of execution. It is a core practice for all projects large and small.

[6] Unfortunately, they also described themselves as not particularly concerned about project leader continuity, which is quite unfortunate in light of overwhelming evidence that continuity is important.

Figure 1.1

When Complex Project Leaders Are Appointed for Their Projects

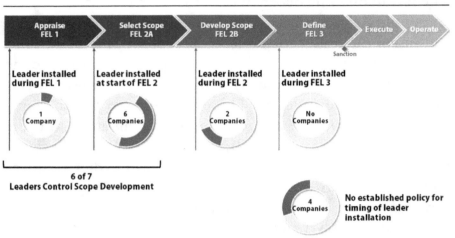

None of the 13 companies routinely wait until the beginning of FEED[7] (FEL 3) to bring the leader onto the project. Four of the companies, including some of the largest, have no established policy around the timing of project leader installation; they sometimes bring the leader on at the start of FEL 2 and others at FEL 2A and still others at the start of FEED. In no case did any respondent suggest that start of execution was ever intended to be the start of the project director's tenure.

The patterns that we find here represent a substantial shift of philosophy in the petroleum industry over the past 20 years. Twenty years ago, the great majority of companies would have responded that the project leader who will lead execution was not installed until FEED at the earliest and frequently not until the start of formal execution.

This change reflects the industry's migration from functionally based and centered project organizations (weak matrix)

---

[7] FEED stands for "front-end engineering design," FEED brings the design of a project to the point that full detailed design can commence. FEL 3 also includes execution planning work by the owner and contractor teams.

to strong, team–based (strong matrix) systems.[8] Two of the 13 companies in our survey have made the switch from function-based to strong matrix just in the past three years in an effort to improve their performance in the face of lower oil prices. Of the 13 companies surveyed, only four indicated that it was normal to have a transition of project leaders during front-end loading. Interestingly, three of those four are very large international companies. None of the independents and only one national company continue to view a turnover of project leadership during or just after FEL as a desirable approach. Twenty years ago, most companies would have described such a transition as normal practice.

We have no doubt, based on 30 years of continuous bench-marking of the process industries,[9] that the transition to strong–matrix systems has improved capital project effective-ness overall.[10] However, it has made relatively little differ-ence in the performance of large complex projects, as there is no discernible time trend of improvement in these projects.

---

[8] In weak–matrix systems, functional managers (e.g., manager for structural engineer-ing, manager for process engineering, manager of estimating, etc.), assign personnel to project teams and maintain a degree of control over those personnel throughout their stint on a project. The functional managers also write the performance reviews for those personnel. This undermines the autonomy and authority of the project directors, which is why this approach is also sometimes called a "weak project manager system." In strong matrix systems, personnel from the needed functions are seconded to the team and then report only to the project manager/director. The functional managers have no control over project management. Hence, these systems are often called "strong project manager systems." Note, however, that some functions are almost always "weak-matrixed" into projects (e.g., legal). Petroleum development projects always involve a degree of "weak-matrixing" because the reservoir (subsurface), drilling, and facilities organizations are never fully integrated.

[9] Included are petroleum production, petroleum refining, mining, metals process-ing, chemicals, pharmaceuticals, pulp and paper, power and infrastructure, and consumer products industries.

[10] The transition to strong-matrix systems has not been without negatives; the decline in owner-project competencies in areas such as construction management and controls has surely been accelerated by the transition to strong-matrix systems.

We believe the failure to improve in these projects can be attributed to a basically flawed process of selecting complex project leaders. The flaws in the selection process are clearly reflected in survey responses discussed earlier. Despite ample opportunity to do so, our respondents made little or no reference to the *leadership* qualities essential to complex project success.

We believe that those who advocate separate project leaders for scope development and execution are misunderstanding the role of the complex project leader. During scope development, the project director is not making the technical decisions of this scope versus that. Instead, the project leader is orchestrating the scope development process, making sure that the pieces of the scope are synchronized properly and ensuring that those outside the project team that can influence the scope (e.g., internal and external stakeholders, regulatory authorities, etc.) are informed and in broad agreement with the scope as it evolves. These activities are not fundamentally different than what the project leader will be doing during execution. Only if one thinks of the project leader as the doer of things, rather than orchestrator, would the skillsets be fundamentally different. We believe the concept of the project leader as doer is flawed on complex projects.

Links to Human Resources

The relationship between corporate human resource (HR) organizations and capital projects is often somewhat tenuous. Project professionals are a small fraction of the people recruited and developed by HR. The profiles and interests of those who will be effective project professionals are usually quite different than those who will be successful in operations or the businesses. In our survey of companies, we inquired

Figure 1.2
The Ties Between Human Resources and Complex Project Leaders Could Be Stronger

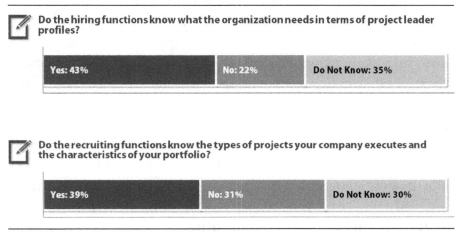

about the ties between HR and complex project leaders. The results are shown in Figure 1.2.

The results suggest that the ties between the projects and HR organizations could and should be strengthened. Most of the respondents were quite senior in their organizations but either didn't know whether the hiring organization understood the desired profile of complex project leaders or were confident they did not. Nearly a third felt that HR did not understand the types of projects the company executes. It is our hope that this book will help forge stronger links between projects and HR going forward as HR's assistance will probably be essential to hiring those who will later become successful complex project leaders.

The Use of Nonoperated Joint Ventures as a Career Development

In Chapter 4 we will discuss one of the key experiential factors that improved the success chances of complex project leaders:

having been assigned to act as a liaison to what is called a non-operated venture (NOV) in the oil industry. Most oil industry projects are joint ventures in which one of the partners is designated as the operating partner that will lead the effort while the others are relegated to watching, approving certain decisions, and sometimes critiquing. The nonoperators typically assign a person or two to liaise with the operator. It is this liaison role we are discussing.

We asked our 13 companies whether they routinely assigned project managers to the liaison role as a development opportunity. Nine of the companies (69%) said they had no such policy, two reported they did sometimes, and the final two said they used the NOVs in this fashion. It appears that in most companies one's appointment to the NOV liaison role is, like many appointments to complex project leadership roles, more a matter of availability than conscious career design. The petroleum industry has the worst track record of any industrial sector in its complex projects with just over one project in five being successful.[11] The irony is that the petroleum industry is almost uniquely poised to use NOV experience to help groom complex project leaders, but is largely unaware that the role is in fact such an opportunity.

WHO SHOULD READ THIS BOOK?

First, anyone with an interest in project management should find this book of interest. If project management is one's chosen career, this book may help the reader understand what qualities he or she should have to pursue leadership of complex projects and, to the extent possible, what qualities need to be developed and nurtured. If one lacks some of the key

---

[11] Merrow, *Industrial Megaprojects*, p. 334.

personality characteristics needed to be a successful complex project leader, a career in project management is not foreclosed. The great majority of project managers are needed on less complex projects. It is important to know realistically where one's talents are best employed.

Second, we hope this book will be read by those who sponsor and are tasked with assigning directors to large complex projects. This book should help guide their decisions of who to put in charge of these critical investments, how a pool of such people should be developed and nurtured, and what critical qualities need to be developed in that group.

Third, we hope those interested in leadership generally find this book of interest. Our research builds on and confirms the work of Daniel Goleman and others about the importance of emotional intelligence to effective leadership. We see no reason that our conclusions about the makeup of successful project leaders should not extrapolate to leaders in all walks of life. When those who have been put into positions of leadership lack certain elements of personality and emotional intelligence, the result is usually disappointment for all involved.

Fourth, those particularly concerned about the leadership of oil and gas production projects should find the book of considerable interest as most of the projects and project leaders that we will discuss are drawn from the petroleum development sector. As those involved in large petroleum projects already know too well, oil and gas projects are particularly prone to failure in the form of large cost overruns, slippage in schedule, and significant shortfalls in production attainment. We believe that many of the failures can and should be understood as failures of leadership. The need for leadership in such projects results from their inherent and unavoidable complexity. The failure to put the right people in place to lead the projects stems from a lack of understanding of what the requirements really are.

Finally, we hope that those in the academic community who study capital projects and their management will see this book as a useful contribution to the literature. We believe this study addresses two weaknesses in the literature directly: (1) a failure to link observations and theory to the outcomes of real projects in a quantitative and systematic way, and (2) the sparseness of the literature in dealing with the personalities and emotional makeup of project leaders and how personality and emotional makeup help shape success and failure.

ORGANIZATION OF THE BOOK

This book is organized into two parts. Part I consists of Chapters 2 through 5 and focuses on the findings of our quantitative study of complex project leadership. Chapter 2 lays out the methodology we followed in the study, including the elements of the survey instrument we employed and how the sample was developed and the nature of the statistical analyses that we performed. In Chapter 2, we also describe the projects associated with the 56 project leaders surveyed. Much of the power of the analysis flows from connecting project leader traits with the results of real projects, so the links between leadership and results can be demonstrated rather than inferred or treated anecdotally. Chapter 2 will be required reading for academic readers and human resource professionals who need to deeply understand how the analysis was approached and executed. Other readers should feel free to skim the chapter, but with the caution that much of the analysis in Chapters 4 and 5 rests on an understanding of the methodology.

Chapter 3 develops and articulates the size and scope of the complex project leader's job. Chapter 3 describes why leadership is essential for complex projects while simple projects can usually succeed with good management alone. Chapter 4 lays out the relationships we found between the personalities, habits of mind, and emotional intelligence of project leaders and project success and failure. Successful leaders are distinctly and clearly different from unsuccessful leaders in a number of important respects. Chapter 5 fashions the links between leaders' personalities and emotional intelligence and the various project tasks they consider of highest importance and therefore to which they devote more of their time and energy. It is the translation from personal traits to actual tasks that forms the causal link between personal traits and success. We complete Chapter 5 by discussing how the tasks considered important and done translate into six project practices that drive success in projects generally and in complex projects in particular.

Part II presents the lengthy interview conversations we had with seven highly successful leaders of complex and difficult projects. Most of these extraordinary people have led multiple successful complex megaprojects totaling over $100 billion in capital investment. We discuss how they came to project leadership as a career, who helped them along the way, and their candid views on what is necessary to make a difficult project succeed. Our hope is to bring life and deeper understanding to some of those dry statistics in Part I. These seven project leaders exemplify many of the traits and connections made theoretically and empirically in Part I.

We conclude by outlining what an improved selection and development process might entail for complex project leaders in any sector of the global economy. We will also suggest how one should approach finding the right project leaders for today's projects by knowing what to look for among the candidates available. Every company has a pool from which to select the right people, but most lack a methodology with which to do so accurately.

PART ONE

In Part I, we explain the methodology behind and the findings of our quantitative study of complex project leadership. Then we examine the size and scope of the complex project leader's job and how it differs from the job of the project manager of simpler projects. This information informs our discussion of the traits that make leaders of complex projects successful. Finally, we look at how the choice of tasks and importance attached to them affect the implementation of six key practices that drive project success. This completes a causal chain that flows from personality to tasks to practices.

CHAPTER 2

METHODOLOGY AND DATA

The study that forms the basis of this book was IPA's[1] second quantitative analysis of the role of personality in project management. The earlier study, completed in 2016, developed some of the key methods used in the current study and demonstrated the efficacy of the remainder.[2] As a matter of essential background, IPA has collected detailed project information on over 20,000 capital projects executed by the petroleum, chemicals, minerals, pharmaceuticals, and electric power and infrastructure industries over the past 30 years. The data have been collected in conjunction with IPA's evaluation and benchmarking of those projects for over 400 firms and government agencies in all parts of the world. The project data have been collected using formal data collection instruments plus extensive face-to-face interviews with the owner teams, contractors, and other project participants. A project is typically evaluated and the concomitant data collected three times: twice prior to authorization and once after the start of beneficial operation. A fourth data collection captures the functionality of the project 12 to 18 months after startup.

---

[1] IPA stands for Independent Project Analysis, Inc., the employer of the authors.
[2] David Purzer, Jonathan Walker, and Kelli Ratliff, "The Project Manager: Pairing the Right Leader with the Right Project," prepared for 26th Annual Industry Benchmarking Consortium Conference, March, 2016.

One of the principal aims of this and other studies in our Competency Evaluation Series is to understand in a systematic and quantitative fashion the relationships between the characteristics of key project personnel and project outcomes.[3] The goal is to understand the personality characteristics, cognitive style, and leadership approaches that promote better project results based on the outcomes of projects. These goals guided our approach.

We selected from our databases a set of 100 recent large and complex projects from 24 major industrial companies, all IPA clients. With the permission of the companies, we sent an electronic survey to the directors of those projects.[4] Fifty-six project leaders completed the survey for us. Although by the standards of surveys this is a very high response rate, we are aware of a bias that was created by the 44 missing surveys: the projects led by those who returned the survey were considerably better than the projects of those who did not. If this response bias had reduced the sample of failed projects too substantially, it would have undermined our ability to evaluate the data. However, even with the bias in the responses, over 40% of the projects had outcomes that ranged from poor to very poor in terms of key outcomes. The expected number of failures would have been over 70% given the characteristics of the projects and the industries from which they were drawn. Given that our primary goal was to compare more and less successful project leaders, the sample bias, while annoying, is not detrimental to achieving our objective.

---

[3] To date (December 2017) we have completed two studies of project managers, one study of construction managers, and have a fourth study in progress on lead engineers.
[4] In megaprojects, the title project director is more common than project manager because there are frequently subprojects that have leaders with the project manager title. In this study, we are focused on the project director/manager who is responsible for leading the overall project.

The survey instrument, which had been vetted with the collection of data from 262 leaders of smaller, less complex projects, employed two well-established tests of personality traits: the Five-Factor Model (widely known as the Big 5) and the Emotional Intelligence Scale. We also employed two additional measures designed by IPA staff, the Hedgehog–Fox Index and the Leadership Style Index. We describe these measures and the survey instrument in the following sections.

THE FIVE-FACTOR MODEL

The Five-Factor Model (Big 5) was developed by L.R. Goldberg (1992) and has been used widely and successfully over the past 25 years.[5] The instrument, which is self-administered, captures key elements of personality. There is a substantial literature that reports studies using the Big 5, including a number of studies of aspiring and practicing engineers, which is the pool from which our project leaders spring. The five factors explored in the Big 5 are:

- Openness
- Conscientiousness
- Extraversion
- Agreeableness
- Neuroticism (emotional stability).

These will be defined and discussed at some length in Chapter 4 as we explore their relationships to project success.

---

[5] L. R. Goldberg, "The Development of Markers for the Big-Five Factor Structure," *Journal of Psychological Assessment* 4 (1992): 26–42. The test is formally referred to as "the 50-item IPIP representation of the Goldberg (1992) markers for the Big-Five factor structure." www.ipip.ori.org.

THE EMOTIONAL INTELLIGENCE SCALE

The Emotional Intelligence Scale (EIS) is a 33-item test developed by Shutte, et al. (1998).[6] Like the Five-Factor Model, it has been used and validated many times. The Emotional Intelligence Scale measures how people use and recognize their own emotions and how well they identify the emotions of others. It was our hypothesis following Goleman and others that effective leadership requires emotional awareness and facility.[7] The emotional intelligence battery of questions is grouped into six separate measures:

1. How well one reads others' emotions
2. How well one reads one's own emotions
3. How effectively one regulates emotions
4. Social skills
5. The ability to use emotions instrumentally
6. Optimism.

Note that in most respects, the Emotional Intelligence Scale is measuring different attributes than the Five-Factor Model, although some of the measures do correlate. As explored later, both the Big 5 and the EIS are helpful in our quest to understand the characteristics of leaders who generate successful complex projects.

THE FOX-HEDGEHOG SCALE

In Isaiah Berlin's 1953 essay, "The Hedgehog and the Fox," there is a hypothesis that the world is divided into two groups:

---

[6] N. S. Schutte, J. M. Malouff, L. E. Hall, D. J. Haggerty, J. T. Cooper, C. J. Golden, and L. Dornheim, "Development and Validation of a Measure of Emotional Intelligence," *Personality and Individual Differences* 25 (1998): 167–177.

[7] Daniel Goleman, *Emotional Intelligence* (New York: Bantam, 1995).

foxes pursue many things, outrun their problems, and see the big picture. The hedgehogs focus on one task at a time, hold their ground, and defend a very small territory very well. We theorized we could take this hypothesis a step further and not only classify a project manager into either group, but tie their individual success as a project manager to the classification. We started with a binary scale: a project manager is either a fox or a hedgehog. However, after further research, we realized it's not as black-and-white as originally hypothesized. People tend to possess qualities from each group. To better understand which group a project manager is more associated with, eight questions were developed with two answers each. Each answer was associated with either the fox classification or the hedgehog. This gave us a gradient scale that we could then use to test our theory.

MEASURING LEADERSHIP STYLE

We developed a series of questions based on Daniel Goleman's *Primal Leadership*.[8] The styles are:

- Visionary
- Coaching
- Affiliative
- Democratic
- Pacesetting
- Commanding.

We designed two questions for each style specifically tailored to the leadership of capital projects. Each question was derived from the explanation of the style from Goleman's

---

[8] Daniel Goleman, *Primal Leadership: How to Lead with Emotional Intelligence* (Cambridge: Harvard Business School Press, 2004).

work. Although a few of the questions we devised were very effective in isolating successful leaders, the overall scales did not work very well for complex project leader assessment. We make use of the questions that did work but make little use of the individual styles.

STATISTICAL METHODOLOGY

We used both parametric and nonparametric statistical techniques to explore the relationships between leader characteristics and project success. Because our primary sample is small ($n = 56$) we set our threshold for statistical significance at .10 rather than our more conventional .05. This means that we accepted a result as being real rather than random if the statistical relationship would occur less than one time in 10 on a random basis with repeated trials.[9] We report our statistical results in the following format: Pr. | statistic | < .xx. The statistic may be a z-score for logit, probit for robust regressions, a chi-square for tabulations, or a t-ratio for parametric tests such as t-tests and least squares regression. So the following, Pr.|t| < .01, would be read "the probability, based on the t-ratio for the variable's coefficient, is less than one chance in 100 that the result would be generated randomly in repeated trials."

MEASURING SUCCESS

Projects have multiple outcomes. Project success is measured against four major outcomes: cost performance, schedule adherence, functionality (production/operability) of the asset,

---

[9] In all cases we used two-tailed tests even if we had a strong prior hypotheses based on the literature or our own prior studies. This means that in most cases on a one-tail basis, our reported results meet or beat the conventional .05 cutoff. Because in most cases we had clearly established hypotheses of the direction of the relationship, a one-tailed test would often have been appropriate.

and construction safety.[10] The first three drive the economic value of the project. Of these three outcomes, cost is usually the most important for large projects because the downside of significant overruns is so large and it is the outcome over which the project leader is seen to have the most control and responsibility. Schedule slip is often driven by the aggressiveness of the original schedule, which is generally dictated by the business, often without much connection to reality. Operability – production against forecast – is a clear measure of quality in chemical processing projects and is very much the accountability of the project leader. In both petroleum and mineral resource projects, however, operability is often driven more by surprises in the reservoir or ore body than by deficiencies in the physical facilities, including wells.

As our primary measure of outcomes, we divided our complex project sample into two groups: those that were successful and those that were not. We used adherence to authorized cost in constant currency and constant scope terms as our primary separator (less than a 10% overrun is considered a success) but subject to correction if the asset did not operate successfully due to facilities or wells problems. In some cases projects were not completed when this book was being written in summer 2017. In those cases we used the status at that point and had to make a judgment as to whether the project would end successfully. We feel confident in these judgments because projects were well into execution and projects generally start to fail early in execution – indeed many have actually failed before they were authorized but no one acknowledges that fact. We

---

[10] For some companies, the safety of the construction effort is the first measure of project management success. Not surprisingly, these tend to be the safest companies. Unfortunately, safety data are not routinely kept in a comparable fashion in oil and gas projects. We, therefore, were unable to use safety as a measure of project success in the current study.

were able to classify 44 of the 56 projects in our sample as successful or not.

THE DATA

To our knowledge, this is a first-of-a-kind research effort that quantitatively links complex capital project outcomes to a project leader's personality and leadership abilities. The end result of this work will be a project leader selection model that can be used to select a specific project leader profile and improve the probability of success of future complex projects. There is a pressing need in both private and public-sector megaprojects to generate a higher rate of success.

To ensure proper use and applicability of the findings and models (and to provide counter to inevitable arguments of, "How could you possibly quantify project leader personality?") we describe below in detail the data used in our study. There are two primary kinds of data: the first are project data that codify all aspects of the project, including project background, characteristics, technical scope details, cost and schedule estimates, and all performance outcome data. The other data are generated by our survey of the project leaders themselves that goes into extensive personal background and personality profiles. We detail both next.

THE PROJECTS DATABASE

As mentioned earlier, we used 56 projects in our study and because of the focus of the study, these are all complex projects as defined in Chapter 1. The average authorization year for the projects is 2011. In other words, the average project in the study was authorized before the recent crash in oil prices. In fact, 75% of the projects in our study were authorized at least a year or more before the decline in prices. This is important as it means that the outcomes of the projects, in most cases, were not influenced by external market conditions and can be much more directly linked to the personality and ability of the leader. It also means that the leaders for the projects were assigned during a period of great activity for the industry.[11] We believe that the companies made the best efforts possible to match the complexity of the project with the skills of the leaders but truly skilled project leaders were in great demand during this time. There is a healthy proportion of the study sample that was authorized in 2014 and only about 10% of the sample was authorized *after* the price crash and naturally these projects are still currently in execution.

The 56 projects in the study were not a random draw; these projects were matched to the project leaders who returned surveys. Naturally, the range of projects, reflected in the asset costs, is reflective of the types of projects the leaders in the study executed. As we will discuss in Chapter 3, complexity is not simply a matter of project cost, although they obviously correlate. The database contains projects that were simple from a technology standpoint but very difficult in other dimensions of complexity, such as stakeholder alignment, local politics, and community involvement. The average estimated asset cost of these projects at the time of authorization was a $3.4 billion, with a large range. The low end of the projects ranged from about $250 million to projects estimated to cost well over $25 billion, with almost three-quarters of the projects estimated at $1 billion or more.

---

[11] As an aside, as of writing of this book, in the aftermath of the oil price crash the petroleum industry projects declined rapidly and many of the project leaders either have taken early retirements, have been made redundant, or have been assigned functional jobs. This does not bode well for the future of the industry because the major projects will surely return as the need to replace reserves drives new projects.

We also had a separate sample of 422 projects executed by the 262 project leaders of small, less complex projects. This was mostly used to understand how different the population of large complex project leaders is from those of small, less complex projects. The average small, less complex project was estimated to cost $200 million with an average authorization year of 2009.

Most of the projects in our complex sample were from the petroleum production industry and the scopes of the projects included the facilities (production processing, and gathering on-shore and subsea, subsea facilities, and pipelines), gas processing facilities and LNG plants, and wells construction, both drilling and completions. The projects covered both on-shore and offshore projects and several chemical megaprojects were included as well. The project leaders represented in the sample sat atop all scopes of work, and the discipline project managers and facilities subproject managers reported to the leader.

The projects in the study have been executed globally as shown in Figure 2.1. Almost a quarter of the projects come from Asia, followed by North America, which is largely off-shore developments in the Gulf of Mexico. Europe and Oceania (Australia and Papua New Guinea) have the next largest group of projects followed by projects in South America and Africa at about 10% each. Projects in Middle East and Former Soviet Union countries round out the sample.

In line with the regional distribution of the projects is the diversity of operators represented in the study sample. Twenty-four global companies are represented as operators in the study, most with multiple projects and project leaders. No company dominates the sample, with the largest representation being only 16% of the sample. National oil companies (NOCs), supermajors, majors, and independents are included as well as several global chemical companies.

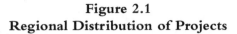

Figure 2.1
Regional Distribution of Projects

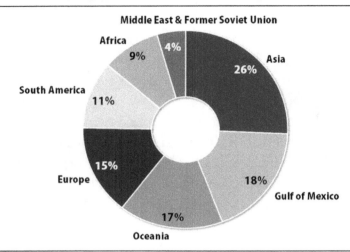

There is often a belief in the petroleum industry that nationally owned oil companies don't aspire to cost competitiveness and capital discipline with the same rigor as supermajors and independents because they have some other goals, such as employment and development of local industry, that are more important than capital competitiveness. It is also believed, incorrectly as it turns out, that supermajors and independents have organizational, process, and project management capabilities superior to NOCs. It was therefore important to this study that the study sample be fully representative of different operator types so that the study findings do have a broad applicability and are not biased. There is no tendency for any particular kind of company to produce better or worse projects in this sample.[12]

---

[12]This same lack of pattern in success and failure by type of company was found in the much larger set of megaprojects examined in Merrow, *Industrial Megaprojects* (2011).

THE PROJECT LEADERSHIP SURVEY

The main objective of our study was to understand the relationship between a project leader's background, experience, personality, and leadership skills and the outcome of the project. To understand our project leaders deeply, we designed an electronic survey instrument that contained over 160 questions designed to probe the leader in the topic areas mentioned above. As shown in Figure 2.2, the questions ranged from descriptive questions to more specific, forced-ranking Likert scale questions that try to get at the leadership style of the leader.

The 160-plus questions were divided into various sections starting with a section about the leaders' background that probed their education, area of study, and any formal and informal leadership training and mentoring they may have received. The next set of questions focused on the experience of the leaders: experience in any capacity on a capital project of varying complexity, experience as project leader,

Figure 2.2
Examples of Descriptive Questions

Please explain your formal leadership experience.

List the 5 tasks you perform most commonly as a project leader.
Think of the specific tasks that consume your time and list those tasks in order of the relative amount of time they consume.

Examples of Likert Scale Questions:

	Strongly Disagree				Strongly Agree
	1	2	3	4	5
When making decisions, I more often rely on the consensus input of my project team than on my own experience.	○	○	○	○	○
As the project leader, I prefer not to delegate decision-making authority.	○	○	○	○	○

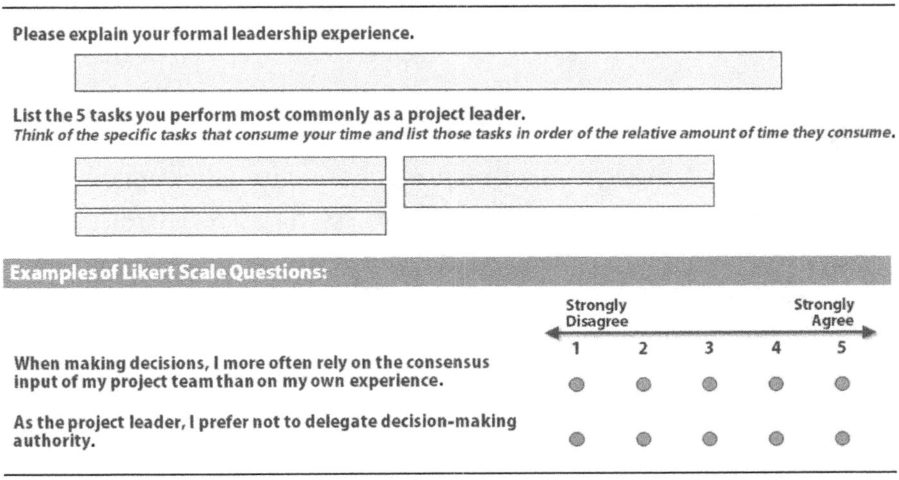

experience in capital projects in other industrial sectors, experience in a nonoperated and/or joint venture setting, as well as their experience on three most recent projects.

We then sought to understand the view of the leaders on what they consider as project leader competencies. For instance, what are the most common tasks they perform in a leadership role, what they believe the most important tasks should be for project leaders. We also solicited their views of the value of process by understanding what tasks they routinely perform, but consider not to be value-adding to their work on a project. And we asked the leaders for their views of what skills and abilities they considered as crucial for success as a leader. We believe that leaders' success is often the result of events, experiences, and people they meet along the way that shape their thinking and views. So some of the questions in the survey were designed to understand people, experiences, and events that were most influential in each leader's development trajectory. After understanding the background, education, and developmental aspects of the leaders the survey asked a battery of questions designed to identify their project leadership style, their general approaches to projects, their personality characteristics, as well as where they sit on the Emotional Intelligence Scale and The Five-Factor Model.

Despite containing more than 160 questions, because of the nature of the questions and responses sought, the survey took only 30 to 40 minutes to complete. As has been mentioned earlier, the survey respondents were not a random lot. In some cases we know that senior managers in some of the companies decided who would complete the survey for us. They generally selected people they considered better-than-average project leaders. Once the survey was completed, our contacts in the company confirmed that the survey took less than an hour to complete in order to proactively address chances of pushback or noncompletion.

Despite this preparation, just over half the surveys were returned but with big differences by company. In some companies every single project leader completed and returned the survey. In others, very few to one leader did. This result, unsurprising to us, was not random. It is directly proportional to the degree of control (or impotence) of the central projects organization. Most oil and gas operators – international oil companies or NOCs – have some sort of a central projects group that oversees capital projects. Yet the degree of influence and control these groups have over personnel and functions involved in projects varies from great to in name only.

So, who are these project leaders? They are 95% male, although women are overrepresented in the successful group. Also, 94% of all leaders have either a bachelor's or master's degree. All of the leaders sampled started their education with a technical background, almost always in engineering. In order of frequency, civil engineering, chemical engineering, and mechanical engineering lead the list of disciplines with petroleum engineering, ocean engineering, and electrical engineering making up most of the rest. We found no differences in performance as a function of the educational background of the respondents.

From a leadership standpoint almost all of the leaders had some sort of formal leadership training – either company-provided training or company-sponsored external training – and adjunct courses and certifications. On average, they have completed about seven projects in a project leader capacity and roughly the same number in other leadership roles. Figure 2.3 shows the distribution of the number of years project leaders have worked in a leadership role on projects that are $1 billion or greater.

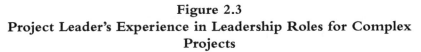

Figure 2.3
**Project Leader's Experience in Leadership Roles for Complex
Projects**

Twenty-seven percent of the project leaders in the study have worked in a capital industry sector other than oil and gas while the remaining 73% of project leaders only have experience in the oil and gas industry. Further, a little more than half of the leaders (56%) have been involved in a project as a nonoperator, while 44% have not. As Chapter 4 will discuss, the last two points are important in the success of a complex project leader.

Eighty-one percent of the project leaders in our study, some of them very senior with many years of experience, have never refused a project that was presented to them for their next assignment. Only 19% of the leaders have actually refused to accept a project assignment. Of those, only three leaders refused the assignment due to a family situation while everyone else refused the assignment because "the fundamentals weren't shaped right and I could not see how I could make any positive difference." That does not mean that the projects done by the 81% of the leaders were all successful. What this means is that of the study sample there were only a handful of leaders who had enough experience (and possibly courage) to see that the opportunity was untenable and they did not want to ruin their reputation, their careers, or their personal capital on what was clearly a situation set up to fail.

How do these leaders develop the nose to sniff out a poorly shaped opportunity? How do they judge a project that they would enjoy being on versus one that would not be fulfilling to them? What are they looking for in an opportunity to judge good versus bad? What is the context – events, roles, past projects, mentors, common tasks – through which they have built this perspective? The survey provides a detailed view on all these questions for every one of the leaders. The surveys provide a comprehensive profile of the leaders, and in many cases we also followed up with the leaders after receiving their responses. Yet, it felt like we were still missing some key developmental events and milestones in the making of the leader. We wanted to deeply understand their developmental journey.

THE FUN PART

To deeply understand all the key events, milestones, experiences, and people that influenced the leaders along their developmental journey and made them what they are, we conducted a series of one-on-one, in-depth (about two to four hours each) interviews with seven highly successful project leaders on a wide range of topics. The topics ranged from their childhood upbringing, influential people in their life, education, early career, and progression to key events that put a rocket on their project leadership trajectory.

These seven leaders, six men and one woman, come from national oil companies, a very large global chemical company,

a major international petroleum company, and three different independent oil and gas operators. They were chosen not
because of their companies but simply because of their standout performance – each one of them has delivered a series of
complex projects (in some cases three back-to-back projects)
successfully. And if there was any lingering doubt about their
true leadership abilities, that is wiped away when you discover
that in every one of their cases team members often left other
jobs and other leaders to come and work with these leaders!
George Simmel (1858–1918), an early sociologist is said to
have written, "Leaders cannot maintain authority unless followers are prepared to believe in the leader." The insights from
these leader interviews are presented as case studies starting
with Chapter 6. All seven graciously allowed us to use their
names and, in all save one case, their affiliations.

CHAPTER 3

THE UNIQUE DEMANDS ON COMPLEX PROJECT LEADERS

Large complex projects are in many respects fundamentally different than their less demanding counterparts. Those differences, which we will discuss below, give rise to the need for a different kind of leader for these projects. As we will discuss in the next chapter, the differences in task requirements for the complex project leader demand a somewhat different personality profile and cognitive style for success.

WHAT MAKES A COMPLEX PROJECT COMPLEX?

Each dimension of complexity discussed below is a continuum rather than a switch. It is always a matter of more or less rather than a matter of simple versus complex. Project complexity correlates with project size and cost. But the relationship is associational, not casual. Some relatively small projects in terms of cost may be highly complex and require complex project management to succeed. Some projects in excess of $1 billion may be relatively simple projects that will succeed with a simple project's approach to management.

Fortunately, the characteristics of a project that will render it relatively simple or relatively complex are usually known early in the project's development life cycle. It is unusual, but not unheard of, for a project to start out simple but become complex along the way. When that occurs, it is almost always due to unexpectedly difficult *shaping*, the third dimension of complexity we discuss below. We cannot recall a situation in which a project started out complex and became simple.

We conceptualize project complexity in three dimensions: scope, organization, and shaping. We will discuss these aspects of complexity below and then discuss how these elements of complexity influence the nature of the work done by the project leader.

The first element of complexity to consider is *scope complexity*. Large projects usually consist of a number of subprojects organized by distinctly different elements of scope. For example, the development of a new oil field will always include a facilities scope of work, a drilling program, and a scope of information production work to develop the approach that will be taken to the drawdown of the reservoir. Often the facilities scope must also be separated into pieces as well: for example, a floating production system, subsea systems, and possibly an export pipeline and on-shore facilities. Note that this sort of scope complexity does not constitute a program. A program is a set of projects, often sequential in nature, that make sense individually but are even more valuable collectively. The sort of scope complexity described in the example above is merely the complexity of a single project in which the individual pieces have no value without every other piece successfully completed.

When new technology is included in the project, scope complexity increases substantially, especially if the new technology is central to the project. We would count scope complexity as high in the case of substantial technological innovation even if the size of the project is not particularly large. One of the added difficulties of large projects is they are more likely to require new technology to be feasible. Introducing new technology in an otherwise complex scope for a large project is the epitome of scope complexity.

But scope complexity may be present even when the scope is quite mundane. For example a long (> 500 km) pipeline project will normally be broken into four or more sections (spreads), pump stations will usually be a separate scope, tricky river or terrain crossings may be another scope, and the terminal and storage yet another. Such a pipeline project can easily end up with 7 to 10 subprojects. Every subproject must be completed successfully or the result has no value.

Scope complexity creates the need for *organizational complexity*.[1] In the examples above, there could be as many as six subteams developing and executing the oil production project work. Each team will have its own sets of required expertise, its own leadership, and often its own culture, vocabulary, and professional ways of working. Each subteam will often draw on the skills of separate engineering and construction/fabrication contractors and vendors. Therefore, even the supply chains will usually be different for different elements of scope. Each subproject manager typically organizes to have a clear line of sight to the performance of team members and to the greatest possible extent the performance of key supply chain players as well. This approach to project organization is common to smaller, simpler projects as well. In the pipeline project example, each of the 7 to 10 subprojects will have a project manager

---

[1] Having a set of subprojects will always give rise to organizational complexity, but subprojects are not necessary for organizational complexity to be present. Companies and agencies that organize their project systems in a functional departmental fashion (i.e., bureaucratically) create organizational complexity that project leaders must cope with in one way or another. In the oil industry, national companies are often organized in a bureaucratic fashion for projects, as are some of the supermajors.

and team and often a separate execution contractor. All must be properly staffed and most importantly, all have to be coordinated to create a coherent asset.

It is hard to overstate the virtues of a management situation in which the effectiveness of all team members is transparent to the project leader. When performance is transparent, the agency problem is mitigated or even eliminated.[2] As complexity grows and as the number of organizations and individuals involved increases, line-of-sight management becomes impracticable and a different style of management becomes essential to success. When managers of complex projects attempt to organize in the line-of-sight style, they work longer and longer hours until they finally yield to the reality and change their approach or burn out in frustration.

Rather than leading a single unified project team with a clear line of sight to all activities, the complex project leader is a leader of leaders. The subprojects are not separate projects; they will often have numerous points of interdependence. The complex project leader must be able to effectively integrate the subproject activities or the whole effort will come unstuck. In a complex project, there are multiple teams and hundreds of professionals working on the project from both the owner and contractor sides of the project. Very few of those professionals will report directly to the project leader, which is good because minding them all would be impracticable.

---

[2] Armen A. Alchian and Harold Demsetz, "Production, Information Cost, and Economic Organization," *The American Economic Review* 62, no. 5 (December 1972): 777–795. The agency problem occurs whenever someone is expected to act in the best interest of another party but can benefit from not doing so. The agency problem is at the core of the difficulty of hiring contractors on complex projects, but that is a subject for another book.

The third element of complexity that attends almost all megaprojects and many smaller complex projects is *shaping complexity*. Shaping is the process by which all of the stakeholders in a project are allocated value and via that allocation process become aligned on the scope of a project during front-end development.[3] We define stakeholders as any organization or individual making an enforceable claim on any of the value of the project.

Stakeholders may be internal or external. An internal stakeholder could be any company function that has some degree of control over the project (hence an enforceable claim) and wants to see the project better reflect its interests or values. For example, operations is always an internal stakeholder on capital projects and often would like to have elements of scope that will make operating the facilities easier while making the project more expensive. Procurement (purchasing) often behaves as both a participant and an internal stakeholder on capital projects. They are a participant in the role of buying equipment and materials for the project, but they also act as an internal stakeholder with goals different from the project to the extent that their key performance indicators (KPIs) are based on being able to account for savings, which pushes them to want a bidding contest on as many items as possible. For at least some items, a bidding contest may not be in the best interests of the project. In many owner organizations, the project director will have little or no control over the procurement organization and must foster cooperation with procurement to succeed. Operations and procurement are merely examples here and rarely the only ones. One of the

---

[3] For extensive discussions of shaping and the shaping process, see Merrow, *Industrial Megaprojects* (2011) and R. Miller and D. Lessard, *The Strategic Management of Large Engineering Projects* (Cambridge, MA: MIT Press, 2000).

best measures of the quality of an owner organization in developing capital projects is the ease or difficulty of aligning the company's or agency's internal stakeholders. The lack of internal cooperation and coherence within the sponsoring organization is one of the biggest challenges for many project directors.

External stakeholders can be a highly variable lot. They may include joint venture partners, governments, local communities, landowners, resource owners, and nongovernmental organizations (NGOs), such as environmental advocates or anti-corruption organizations. Projects with complex scopes usually have complex permitting and regulatory processes. Each permitting authority and regulator is an external stakeholder in the project.

For a variety of reasons, large complex projects are likely to have large and varied sets of stakeholders:

- Large projects are more likely to be financed by joint ventures instead of single firms and often the joint-venture partners bring external lenders who become stakeholders.
- Large and complex scopes of work are likely to entail more regulatory and approval authorities.
- Large and complex scopes of work are more likely to have adverse effects on local communities and the environment, thereby triggering interest of local groups and NGOs.
- And, of course, large complex projects require vast piles of money; piles of money draw politicians in much the same way as piles of manure draw flies.

Large and varied sets of stakeholders create an array of challenges for project leaders. At least some, and too often all, of the management of stakeholders falls on the project director.

Each stakeholder has the ability to disrupt a project (otherwise they would not have enforceable claims) and, therefore, must be managed. Whenever the stakeholder set is varied, it is all but certain that they will have conflicting objectives. For example, when a regulator or a local community or an NGO want a project changed in some way to better match their objectives, it is a safe bet to assume their changes will increase the cost of the project rather than decrease it. That puts them at logger-heads with the investors in the project. Almost a third of the joint venture projects in our sample reported sharp conflicts between the partners during the development and execution of the project.

Internal stakeholders are present in all projects, but in smaller projects it is unusual for the stakeholder set to be large and contentious. In large complex projects it is the norm. Complex projects involve almost all functions in a modern corporation: commercial, legal, purchasing, compliance, investor relations, finance, as well as the technical functions and operations. Despite necessary involvement in projects, many internal stakeholders know precious little about how projects actually work and often have little incentive to learn and to cooperate. (How many project-savvy lawyers do you really know?)

These three dimensions of complexity – scope, organization, and shaping – are not independent, although they can potentially exist in any mix. For example, it is unusual to find a project with very complex scope that is not also organizationally complex because the scope complexity drives the need for organizational complexity. A project with a complex scope is more likely to be large and draw more stakeholders, both internal and external, that make the shaping challenges greater. But as the complexity grows in any of the three dimensions, the burdens on the project leader increase. Equally important, the nature of the project leader's job changes in important ways.

HOW COMPLEXITY CHANGES THE LEADERSHIP REQUIREMENTS

Scope complexity requires that the project leader has a broad understanding across a number of technologies. Nowhere is this more apparent than in petroleum development projects, which for that reason provide a good example of the scope/knowledge interaction.

A petroleum development project typically brings together five major groups within the lead company:

1. Reservoir appraisal and petroleum engineering
2. Wells drilling and completions
3. Facilities engineering
4. Operations
5. Commercial.

The project leader is typically drawn from facilities engineering, but if facilities engineering is all that the project leader understands, failure will surely follow. The challenge for the petroleum development project leader is to integrate the work of all five organizations into a coherent whole. That requires a broad understanding of everyone's work, not just facilities engineering. The understanding does not necessarily have to be detailed, but it does need to be comprehensive in the sense that the implications of each organization's work for the work of every other group have to be understood correctly. Even the facilities portion of the project alone may have two to five distinct scope areas that have to be integrated. The point is scope complexity forces the leader to know a lot about a lot of things because it is the integration of things that defines the complex project leader's job.

Organizational complexity may present even greater challenges. The work of a project manager in noncomplex projects consists primarily of defining the work of the relatively small owner team and supervising contractors and vendors. Most project managers take an active role in many aspects of the project's development and execution. They meet with members of their team and key players from the contractor's team once or twice a week. They usually move to the offices of the prime contractor and then move with the project to the field. The organization of the project is a straightforward team organization with line-of-sight from the project manager to every core team member. This basic, single-team form of organization is known (and mostly loved) by every manager of industrial projects. The problem is that the line-of-sight organization does not scale to complex projects and attempting to impose the approach on complex projects is a certain recipe for failure.

Organizational complexity changes the leader from a leader of doers to a leader of leaders. Being a leader of leaders is a very different kind of management activity than being a leader of doers. As a leader of doers, the project manager can be quite transactional in style, laying out task assignments, keeping careful track of performance on those tasks, and intervening as needed to correct and adjust. If the business objectives were clear and unchanged and the front-end work done thoroughly, the usual noncomplex project is a *management* challenge, but rarely a *leadership* challenge. The range of talents and knowledge for the simple project leader can be relatively narrow without unduly harming the project. Generally, the simple project does not require the articulation of a nuanced vision of the endeavor because the requirements are already clearly delimited.

When a project manager takes on his first complex project, it may be the first time he has ever had to think seriously about how to organize a project. A host of new questions immediately arises:

- How should the subproject leaders report?
- How is upward information flow fostered?
- How is information flow between subprojects facilitated and controlled?
- How large a staff is needed in the project center?
- What functions and activities should be located in the center?

Organizational complexity forces a conventional project manager to fundamentally change his or her approach to communication and supervision. The communication must be at a higher, more visionary level and supervision must give way to leading rather than directing.

Finally, *shaping complexity* adds a whole realm of work that is far afield from the technical educations of the typical project manager: politics, diplomacy, negotiation, and economics. The central activity for the project leader in shaping is stakeholder management. But the project leader has no line management authority over any of those stakeholders – internal or external. The test of leadership is not gaining the cooperation of people whose livelihoods are based on your approval: the test of leadership is getting people who don't have to agree to follow willingly and even enthusiastically. In that sense, the project manager in charge of a complex project is a manager in name only and a project leader in reality.

Figure 3.1
Managing Up, Over, and Down

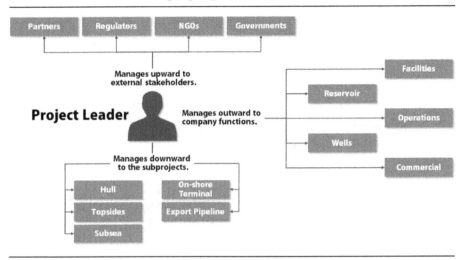

The challenge associated with complex project leadership is illustrated by example in Figure 3.1. The figure represents a rather ordinary petroleum development project in terms of leadership. There are three distinct levels of management involved. First, there is the usual challenge of managing downward. There are often three to five subprojects, each with its own project manager. The project director is responsible for seeing that those facilities projects are fully integrated with respect to technology, scope, and time.

The second level is managing outward to the other groups within his company or agency who must be involved in the development or execution of the project. These are some of the internal stakeholders. Each of those groups has its own culture and its own specialized vocabulary. Sometimes the leaderships of the other groups foster cooperation, but frequently they foster internal competition, rivalry, and blame. In those cases, the effective project leader has to induce or cajole enough cooperation or the project will fail. Often, there are other functions, such as legal, purchasing, safety, and others that are "weak matrixed" into the project and must also be induced to cooperate.

The third level is managing upward to the external stakeholders. In companies with strong systems for managing complex projects, stakeholder management is done by a number of people, not just the project leader alone. But the project leader almost always has a central role and that role often expands during execution. Stakeholder management requires a set of soft skills that would often challenge even an experienced diplomat.

If the complex project leader cannot effectively manage outward to internal stakeholders and upward to external stakeholders, that failing quickly becomes apparent to those working below as the project gets caught up in politics. To those below at the "workface" the most important job of the project leader is to manage things such that they can do their work without political interference. If the leader cannot provide protection from the opportunistic vice president or quarreling partners or the local officials, those below in the project hierarchy will lose confidence and the project leader's tenure is in doubt as well as the project's success.

Our point is a simple one: the complex project leader's job is really quite difficult and the skill set required to navigate this position well is quite remarkable. There is no reason to expect that the effective leader of simple projects will end up as an effective leader of complex projects. It is not a matter of scaling up; it is a fundamental difference in kind. Therefore, we should be unsurprised that the work needs a different personality profile. Yet the principal way that complex project leaders are chosen is willy-nilly from the pool of managers of simpler projects. It is the goal of this book to help correct or at least mitigate that problem.

LEADERSHIP IS MORE IMPORTANT FOR COMPLEX PROJECTS

As projects become more complex, the leadership role not only expands, it becomes progressively more important to project success. The complex project has many more paths to failure than a simple project. There are many more groups and individuals who can derail a complex project, and it is less likely that all those groups and individuals are fully aligned around the definition of success of the project. Even if they are aligned around the definition and need for success, they may have a very different notion of how that success can and should be achieved. In a complex project, the leader's primary responsibility is to create alignment around a single vision of how the project should evolve. The more complex the project becomes the less likely that unified vision is actually present and the more essential the leader's role becomes.

The support for our conclusion that leadership is more important for complex projects comes from examining the effects of turnover in the project director/leader position for complex projects versus their more straightforward counterparts. At IPA we have quantitatively explored the effects of leadership continuity on project results for 30 years. Contrary to what one might imagine, very few replacements of owner project directors occur for cause. Only in unusual cases are owner project leaders removed because of poor performance. Most are replaced for convenience of one sort or another.

The most common reason for project leader replacement is simply rotational assignment. Many companies have rules that limit overseas assignments to 24 to 36 months, after which the

Figure 3.2
Project Leader Turnover Damages All Outcomes

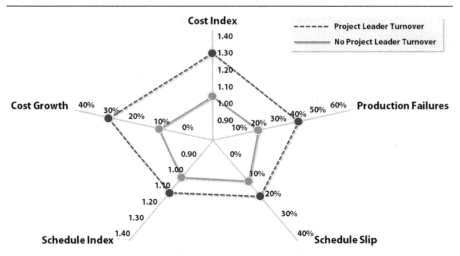

person must be reassigned. Given that most complex projects last over four years in execution, turnover of the leadership when these rules are enforced is inevitable. The second most common reason is that the project director is burned out and asks to be replaced. This occurs almost exclusively on highly schedule-accelerated projects.[4] The third cause of project leader turnover in complex projects is retirement. Because companies often do not realize the importance of project leader continuity, they often assign project leaders who, due to their age or tenure, have little or no chance of actually completing the project. Figure 3.2 shows why this is a very poor decision.[5]

---

[4] Schedule acceleration is measured as the ratio of the execution time promised at authorization divided by the industry average execution time for equivalent projects.

[5] One of our reviewers raised a fascinating point here: if a project leader knows that he or she will not see a project through to the end, can that create a kind of internal agency problem? The answer is clearly yes. For example, if one is leading only the scope development phase, there is a completely different calculus than if one will have to live with that scope right through to the startup of the project.

Figure 3.2 shows five important outcomes of complex projects. The data are drawn from over 300 megaprojects that were reported in Merrow (2011). Cost growth is overruns measured in constant currency/constant scope terms. The cost index measures the cost effectiveness of the project on a location–adjusted basis, in other words adjusted cost per unit of product. The production failures did not operate successfully for at least two years after mechanical completion. Schedule slip is measured as the ratio of the achieved execution schedule to the schedule promised at full-funds authorization, and the schedule index is the amount of execution time required relative to industry average.

Turnover of leadership in complex projects is devastating to the economics of the project. The projects with no turnover of project leadership lost about 50% (median) of their promised net present value (NPV) between authorization and realization, but about 60% were still profitable. The projects with turnover lost 105% (median) of promised NPV and less than a quarter were still profitable.[6]

WHY IS LEADERSHIP MORE IMPORTANT IN COMPLEX PROJECTS?

As discussed earlier, complexity makes the project leader's job bigger, more varied, and more difficult. But it also changes the nature of the job in a more fundamental sense. Complex projects are by their nature fragile. Complexity means that the number and variety of failure modes increases significantly vis-à-vis simpler projects.

To use a metaphor, the less complex project manager is the leader of a small rock band. The leader decides what the band

---

[6] These results were simulated using the IPA Asset Economic Simulator.

will play next but, if the band is skilled and rehearsed, not a great deal of real-time leadership is needed; everybody knows their part. Even without rehearsal, they may improvise in a way that achieves success.

The complex project leader is conducting a symphony orchestra. For many of the musicians and perhaps even the conductor, this is the first public performance of this piece for them. Although they may be skilled musicians, most of the members of the orchestra have never played together before. Their only rehearsal was what we call front-end loading. The orchestra conductor, like the complex project leader, is the glue that not only binds the orchestra together during the performance, but is the source of their vision and inspiration as they perform. He keeps the various sections of the orchestra (read subprojects) synchronized and making music rather than noise.

CHAPTER 4

THE TRAITS AND SKILLS OF EFFECTIVE PROJECT LEADERS

In Chapter 3 we established the remarkable breadth of the complex project leader's job as one of managing upward, outward, and down. In this chapter we will discuss the personalities and decision-making styles of complex project leaders. We are particularly interested in the personality profiles that would make leaders more likely to successfully execute their difficult jobs. We also seek to understand how the profiles of successful leaders may differ from less successful leaders and how successful leaders differ from the larger pools of project managers and engineers from which they are usually drawn.

ORGANIZATION OF THIS CHAPTER

This section focuses on exploring and establishing the links between four traits of project leaders and the success of their projects. These building blocks of project leadership are shown in Figure 4.1. The reader may object to our exclusion of training from this list. It was not an oversight. Rather, it reflects the fact that every one of our 56 project leaders reported quite a lot of formal and informal training in the period leading up to their taking on a megaproject. In any event, it is widely accepted in the project management community (and our observation as well) that virtually all good training in project management is on the job.

Figure 4.1
Building Blocks of Project Leadership

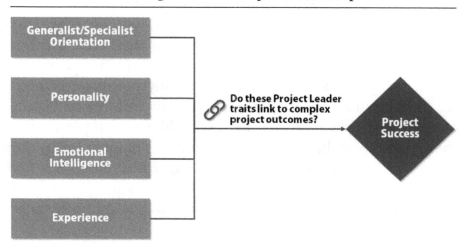

We will start the chapter with our measurement of the generalist/specialist distinction, which we call the hedgehog/fox scale. We then use the Five-Factor Model (Big 5) to measure personality and the Emotional Intelligence Scale to see whether emotional fluency is important to complex project leadership. We end the chapter with an examination of whether particular kinds of experiences earlier in a career help shape successful leaders. This chapter is full of statistical relationships and references back to the literature, which are likely beyond boring to a nonacademic audience. But we believe this background development is essential to appreciating the next chapter in which the causal train from personality and emotional intelligence to concentration on the right task to strong project practices is traced out. Also, if one wishes to use psychological measures to help select the right people for project leadership positions, it is necessary as a matter of fairness and law to demonstrate reliable statistical relationships between these measures and actual project outcomes.

THE HEDGEHOG AND THE FOX

The Greek poet Archilochus (seventh century BC) says "a fox knows many things, but a hedgehog knows one important thing." Isiah Berlin, in his 1953 essay, uses the hedgehog/fox distinction as a way of classifying philosophers.[1] But the distinction can be usefully applied to any profession. There are those who like to dig very deeply into some aspect of their profession versus those who like to sample every-thing – the specialist versus the generalist. The specialist is the hedgehog; the sampler is the fox. Being a hedgehog or a fox is neither good nor bad. But the differences in approach to decisions may make one more or less well-suited to particular work.

As described in Chapter 2, we measured the hedgehog–fox distinction with a battery of eight questions designed to mea-sure the project leaders' style of management. Recall, again from Chapter 2, that we have two samples: a general group of project managers of generally smaller and less complex projects and our sample of 56 complex project leaders. The distributions of project managers overall and complex project managers are shown in Figure 4.2. A score of 4 is neutral on the measure, while lower numbers are more specialist in their orientation and higher numbers are more generalist. Overall, the leaders of complex projects ($n = 56$) are a much "foxier" group than a larger sample ($n = 262$) of managers of less com-plex projects. The median complex project leader scored a median of 6 on the 1 to 8 scale, while the less complex project managers scored 4 with a nearly normal distribution around the mean of 4. The difference between the two groups is sta-tistically significant (Pr. $|z| < 0.02$).

---

[1] Isiah Berlin, *The Hedgehog and the Fox* (London: Weidenfeld & Nicolson, 1953).

Figure 4.2
Hedgehog–Fox Scale: Project Managers vs. Complex Project Leaders

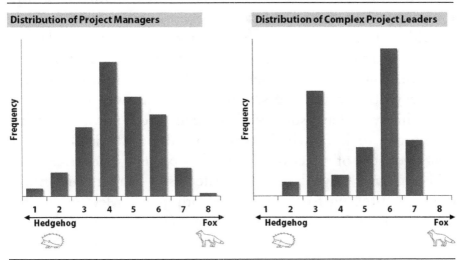

The general result suggests that the companies making selections of leaders for larger, more complex projects favor foxes over hedgehogs or that hedgehogs somehow find themselves blocked in career advancement. (It is also possible that hedgehog project managers self-select out, but that seems less likely because complex project leadership is viewed as the highly desirable top of the profession by project managers. Very few would actually turn such an assignment down.) Note, however, that the complex leader group has a nearly bimodal distribution. This strongly suggests that the selection of generalists is not being made in a systematic fashion by our industrial clients. A number of people who are more specialist by nature are making it into the complex leader ranks. But how do they fare?

Using the better-versus-worse project outcomes distinction defined in Chapter 2, we find that the foxier complex project managers are significantly more likely to have successful projects $(Pr. | X^2 | < .016)$. The single question that best separates the more successful leaders from the others was the question: "When a significant problem arises on a project, would you rather (a) identify a solution quickly and plan its implementation in detail, or (b) try to identify all potential solutions and then implement your chosen solution quickly?" Those who selected the second (foxier) answer were much more likely to have successful projects. We believe this habit of mind – to look widely across possibilities – is absolutely characteristic of successful complex project leaders. As we will see later in this chapter, successful leaders are more open to listening to the views of others than less successful leaders. Divergent points of view are valued by the successful project leader. The difference on the hedgehog/fox scale between the general population of project managers and the complex leaders set was amplified by the sample bias among the complex projects where more successful project leaders tended to be included by the companies. A random sample would have had more unsuccessful project managers and the difference would be less pronounced. Nonetheless, this reinforces our conclusion that the companies are not making effective choices *ex ante*.

The literature on team functionality and effectiveness supports the criticality of listening to the creation of effective teams.[2] The willingness to listen is an essential element to create psychological safety, in which team members feel they can contribute information without fear of ridicule and embarrassment. Several years ago the Google Corporation did an exhaustive study of team performance and found that teams in which psychological safety was high outperformed

---

[2] Amy Edmondson, "Psychological Safety and Learning Behavior in Work Teams," *Administrative Science Quarterly* 44, no. 2 (June 1999): 350–383.

Figure 4.3
Fox versus Hedgehog: *Foxes Deliver on Cost*

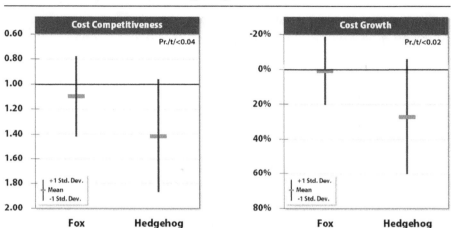

all others, even if the individuals on the team were less accomplished.[3] The successful teams permitted all team members to talk about the same amount in their meetings and were characterized by high social sensitivity, or what we will later in this chapter discuss as emotional intelligence.

Figure 4.3 shows quantitatively how foxes and hedgehogs diverge on the key outcome of cost. The foxes delivered projects that were both more cost effective and much less prone to overruns than the hedgehogs. Perhaps even more important, the variation around both outcomes is much less for the foxes. That indicates that the foxes were better able to keep their complex project under control. To quote one of the project leaders, "My job is to keep this darned thing [the project] from flying off into space. I'm like that little boy sticking his fingers in the dike." Mixed metaphors aside, the language perfectly defines activities that the fox would find

---

[3] Charles Duhigg, "What Google Learned from Its Quest to Build the Perfect Team," *New York Times Magazine*, February 25, 2016.

interesting and perhaps even fun, but the hedgehog would find very uncomfortable and even distasteful. Note that the projects run by more specialist-oriented leaders suffered an average overrun of 25% in constant currency and constant scope terms.

The generalist foxy style is associated with success because it better fits the complexity of the projects. The habit of mind of being interested in everything facilitates the foxy project leader moving across diverse topics routinely. In the morning she may be entertaining skeptical partners or NGOs, at midday her focus may shift to coordinating with the drillers, even if they sometimes seem extraterrestrial, the afternoon may be devoted to coaching project team members who are struggling to get their work completed, and the evening means reporting back to her boss who is 12 time zones away and interested only in cost and schedule and none of her problems. The typical complex project leader rarely has two similar days in a row. The mix of work and concerns is constantly changing. If one would really rather concentrate on a single facet of the job, the constantly changing mix of requirements and the inability to really dig in on a subject of concern would tend to take a heavy emotional toll. To the fox, that is all part of the fun. In our sample, the foxes have about four more years of experience than the hedgehogs. We attribute that entirely to the weeding out process as hedgehogs discover they are (or are discovered to be) poor fits for the position.

When we interviewed some of the best-of-the-best complex project leaders we discovered something curious: although all embraced a generalist style, most had started their careers as specialists. Furthermore, they were very success-ful specialists. They did not leave their specialties because they were not succeeding; they left because they were feeling constrained. They had proven to themselves that they could be a very good electrical engineer, or chemical engineer, or petroleum engineer. Now they needed to prove something more and preferably something with more interaction with the world's most complicated creatures.

We do not know whether some people change on the hedgehog/fox scale over time, but we do know that moving from a specialist to a generalist did occur often among our best project leaders. This will surely be important for those responsible for orchestrating the career paths of major project leaders to understand. The pool of younger technical specialists in a company contains within it some successful specialists who can later become the best project leaders in the company.

The superior performance of foxes implies that companies needing to develop complex project leaders need to put candidates for that group into positions and assignments that broaden their horizons to see who thrives and who does not. Those who seek out and do well in broader assignments are likely to be better candidates for complex project leadership later. At the end of this chapter we will discuss the role that experience can play in creating better project leaders. We suspect that one of the problems that organizations have in finding project leaders is that on the technical side of the organization, specialists are often (quite reasonably) preferred to generalists. Specialists, after all, get the technical work of the organization done. Technical functional managers are not likely to identify future complex project leaders within their ranks for fear of losing them unless they are specifically incentivized to do so because most of these future leaders are good at the technical specialist side of their job. They just aren't satisfied.

Foxiness alone does not make a strong leader, and being a fox rather than a hedgehog explains only about 15 to 20% of the variation in success, but it clearly helps (Pr. $|z| < .004$,

Pr.|t|.002).[4] So let's explore other attributes of personality and experience that may contribute to leadership success.

THE PERSONALITIES OF COMPLEX PROJECT LEADERS

Why should we care about exploring any relationships between personality and project leader performance? The simple and persuasive answer is because personality is one of the characteristics of people that employers really cannot change. We can train and we can provide broad generalist career paths, but if personality plays a significant role in success, we need to select the right people or we will forever be trying to force square pegs into round holes.

As discussed in Chapter 2, we employed two well-established tests to provide insights into the personalities of our project leaders: the Five-Factor Model (also known as the Big 5) and the Emotional Intelligence Scale. We augmented these two tests with a battery of questions that IPA developed to understand the leadership styles of the respondents and how they typically made project management decisions. We then linked these various measures to how well or how poorly projects turned out. We are, of course, not suggesting that the project leader is the only factor that drives project outcomes. One of the characteristics of complex projects is that they have lots of ways to fail. But we have established that project leadership is an important element in success, especially for complex projects. Now we want to understand the qualities – the right stuff in Tom Wolfe's parlance – that constitute good project leaders for these difficult ventures.

---

[4] McFadden's pseudo-R^2 from the probit regression is .15 while the R^2 from a least squares is .20. While neither statistic is precisely right, 15 to 20% is likely to be the proper range.

Understanding the Baseline: Personality Characteristics of Engineers

Most of the studies of engineers and other technically trained professionals compare college students separated by their major field of study. Are students representative of more experienced practitioners? One of the important characteristics of the Five-Factor Model scales is that the mean scores and standard deviations change very little as a function of age with the possible exception of conscientiousness, which may rise with age.[5] Therefore, studies of college students, who are the most easily available subjects to academics, are useful for understanding personality characteristics of those later in their careers. We were able to find only one study employing a version of the Big 5 that studied mid-career engineers, Van Der Molen et al. (2007), but the study was rather limited with respect to size and breadth of subjects.[6] However, we also found a very useful systematic comparison of students by academic majors using the Big 5.[7]

There is a pervasive stereotype that paints the engineer as an introverted nerd. That stereotype is largely debunked by virtually all of the studies of engineers using the Big 5. The typical engineer is in fact rather extraverted and outgoing. No study finds significant differences in the level of neuroticism in engineers relative to those choosing other professions. Most studies find that, as a group, engineers tend to be rather emotionally stable, not subject to significant mood swings, and

---

[5] See S. Srivastava, S. John, O. P. Gosling and J. Potter, "Development of Personality in Early and Middle Adulthood," *Journal of Personality and Social Psychology* 84 (2003): 1041–1053.

[6] H. T. Van Der Molen, H. G. Schmidt, and G. Kruisman, "Personality Characteristics of Engineers," *European Journal of Engineering Education* 32, no. 5 (2007): 495–501.

[7] Anna Vedel, "Big 5 Personality Group Differences Across Academic Majors: A Systematic Review," *Personality and Individual Differences* 92 (2016): 1–10.

not prone to excessive worrying. Studies differ with respect to how engineers score on the Agreeableness scale, but in no case are the differences between population means large. We will return to the agreeableness scale later because a nuanced look does reveal some important attributes of successful leadership. Engineers as a group, however, differ significantly and systematically on two of the Big 5 scales: conscientiousness and openness.

Engineers Are Conscientious

One of the clearest traits of engineers as a group is their level of conscientiousness. On the Big 5 scale of conscientiousness engineers describe themselves as like the Boy Scouts – always prepared. They like to be neat, thorough, and get things done right away rather than procrastinating. For those skeptical of whether these tests work, we found that the time from receipt of our survey to completion correlates very nicely with how the project leaders scored on the conscientiousness scale. Lievens et al. (2002) found that aspiring engineers ($n = 308$) were more conscientious than any other group save for aspiring lawyers.[8] Kline and Lapham report engineers as the highest of any group on the Five-Factor Model conscientiousness scale. The quality of being conscientious is one aspect of the engineering stereotype that is correct.

Engineers are Not Very Open

In the Five-Factor Model, openness measures a person's willingness to entertain new ideas. Those who score highly in

---

[8] F. Lievens, P. Coetsier. F. DeFruyt, and J. DeMaeseneer, "Medical Student Personality Characteristics and Academic Performance: A Five Factor Model Perspective," *Medical Education* 36, no. 11 (2002): 1050–1056.

openness describe themselves as full of ideas and having a conceptual bent. Those high on openness tend to be reflective, which is not to say introverted. Those who are less open are less interested in the abstract and more interested in the practical and down-to-earth. Lievens et al. (op. cit.) report that engineering students are less open than any other group studied and that the differences are often large and routinely statistically significant. Kline and Lapham (1992) similarly put engineers at the bottom on the openness scale.[9] These results probably fit our overall impression of engineers as practical problem-solvers rather than pie-in-the-sky thinkers. But it also suggests that as a group, engineers are not very comfortable with ambiguity and uncertainty. They are probably less likely to entertain novel ideas on a subject and perhaps less likely to solicit as many points of view as possible. Their scores on the conscientious scale tend to reinforce the dislike of ambiguity – their preference as a group is for order and certainty. We believe that is very important because complex project leadership is an activity fraught with uncertainty and messiness.

COMPARING SIMPLER AND COMPLEX PROJECT LEADER PERSONALITIES

In Chapter 2 we explained that we have two samples of industrial project leaders: a sample of 262 leaders of small, simple projects and a sample of 56 leaders of very large and complex projects. Table 4.1 compares the two samples on the Five-Factor Model personality inventory. The remarkable thing about the two samples is that they are virtually identical,

---

[9] P. Kline and S.L. Lapham, "Personality and Faculty in British Universities," *Personality and Individual Differences* 13, no. 7 (1992): 855–857.

Table 4.1

Comparison of Project Leaders

Big 5 Attribute	Less Complex Project Managers		Complex Project Leaders	
	Mean	Standard Deviation	Mean	Standard Deviation
Open	50	7.5	49	6.8
Agreeable	52	7.5	52	7.4
Extraverted	43	8.7	41	8.2
Neurotic	41	7.6	42	7.4
Conscientious	53	7.1	53	7.1

both in the mean scores and the variation around those scores despite having no overlap of membership.[10] The complex project leaders are clearly part of the same population.

What this demonstrates is that industrial companies are paying no heed to personality characteristics as they select project managers for their most difficult projects. On the Emotional Intelligence Scales we find exactly the same null results. Simple and complex leader scores are indistinguishable. The complex leaders then appear to be a random draw of smaller project leaders based on personality and emotional intelligence. We know from years of observation that companies believe they are selecting the best of midsized project managers to take on their larger more difficult projects. So what this suggests is that success as a midsized project leader is not a good predictor of success in complex projects. As we will see in the next section, however, personality really does matter when it comes to effective leadership in complex projects.

---

[10] From a methodological viewpoint, the similarities of the two samples are encouraging for the stability of the Five-Factor Model results.

THE PERSONALITY PROFILES OF SUCCESSFUL LEADERS

We turn our attention now to comparing the personality traits of project directors who led successful projects to those whose projects were not successful. Our focus is now solely on the complex projects. Recall that about 60% of our complex projects were successful based on adherence to budget and functionality of the asset facilities.

Extraversion

There are no meaningful differences between the best and the worst project leaders on the Extraversion scale or any of its components. As shown in Table 4.1, at just over 40 on this scale, project leaders overall are about in the middle.[11] The successful project leaders are slightly less extraverted at the median. No component of the Extraversion scale even approaches statistical significance in separating the more and less successful project leaders. The distribution on this scale is virtually normal with no skewness.

Neuroticism

The differences on this scale between the successful and unsuccessful are not statistically different, but the two groups do not distribute themselves in the same way. The successful group is more uniformly emotionally stable with a normal distribution around the mean. But the unsuccessful group

---

[11] The Big 5 scales are built from 10 questions each with all questions having a scale that ranges from 1 to 7 with 4 being neutral. A score of 40 would average exactly neutral across all 10 questions. Scores above 40 progressively diverge from neutral toward more extraverted, less neurotic, more agreeable, and so forth. Scores below 40 have the opposite effect. For the 50-item inventory used in this study, there were no norms for engineers based on the same inventory available.

has about half of the sample that is decidedly more neurotic and the other half that is decidedly less neurotic. In short, the unsuccessful sample has a clearly bimodal distribution. Despite the relatively small sample ($n = 33$) such a bimodal distribution is not expected. Suffice it to say, the overall group is quite stable emotionally, which is very much in keeping with what the literature tells us about engineers generally. We will see in Chapter 5 that the more neurotic project leaders are likely to avoid certain types of important leadership tasks while the more emotionally stable will take those tasks on, if not always with pleasure.

Conscientiousness

Conscientiousness characterizes all project leaders. The more and less successful project leaders do not differ on this attribute of personality. In general, because engineers tend to be a conscientious lot, selecting project leaders on this trait should not be difficult. It turns out that more conscientious project leaders are more willing to take on some difficult tasks, which is almost a definition of conscientiousness!

Agreeableness

More successful project leaders describe themselves overall as more agreeable than their less successful counterparts (Pr. $|z|$ .02). It is very important, however, that we understand that agreeableness does not mean they go along. Agreeableness measures the extent to which a person is concerned about the welfare, especially the emotional welfare, of others. This reflects a leadership style that values teamwork.

Although successful project leaders are more agreeable on most of the individual measures of agreeableness, there is only one on which they are much more likely to respond affirmatively than their less successful colleagues: "I make people feel at ease." Fifty-two percent of successful leaders describe that statement as fairly or completely accurate while only 22% of unsuccessful leaders do (Pr.$|z| < .04$). The emotional skill of putting people at ease strikes us as particularly important for the leaders of complex projects because there are so many different kinds of people with whom they must work effectively and most of those people do not have to cooperate if they are not inclined to do so. Many complex projects entail close working relationships with people from a variety of cultural, religious, and linguistic backgrounds. The ability to put people at ease is a particularly useful skill in such situations.

Openness

The Big 5 personality trait that best describes successful project leaders is openness (Pr.$|z| < .015$). Openness in the Big 5 measures the degree to which one is comfortable entertaining new ideas, tends to think abstractly, and perhaps even the extent to which one is a little quirky. Every item on the Big 5 openness scale points toward more successful project leaders being more open. Openness means that successful project leaders are more likely to listen carefully and consider all points of view. Recall from our earlier discussion that engineers as a group tend to score low on this scale. However, in both of our samples of project leaders, the more and less complex tended to score higher than normal on the openness scale. Our hypothesis is that engineers who choose project management as a career are not satisfied with a career pursuing their engineering specialty and prefer instead a career that is more people and team oriented while still drawing on their technical skills. Those who make it to the top of their profession as successful project managers tend to be those who are most comfortable with the uncertain nature of capital projects. Interestingly, however, it is only in complex projects that the relationship between openness and success is clear. That difference tells us that the personality characteristics that are important in complex projects may not be particularly important for the success of simpler projects.

It is not just the openness scale on the Big 5 that relates strongly to complex project success. Questions in the fox/hedgehog, emotional intelligence, and leadership scales that tap some attribute of openness all have significant relationships to project success.

EMOTIONAL INTELLIGENCE AND PROJECT LEADERSHIP

As discussed in Chapter 2, Emotional Intelligence measures how well one identifies, regulates, and employs emotions in oneself and recognizes emotions in others. Given that emotions, which stem from our animal selves, are crucial in social life, the leader who is better able to use, recognize, and control emotions has a material advantage. The ability of a leader to evoke emotional responses in others and to understand his or her emotional reactions to situations is obviously important to effective leadership. Daniel Goleman makes the key point that emotional intelligence is quite different than being generally intelligent, which is why many very smart people utterly fail in leadership roles.[12]

As discussed in Chapter 2, the 33-item Emotional Intelligence test is grouped into six scales. Table 4.2 shows how

---

[12]Daniel Goleman, "What Makes a Leader," *Organizational Influence Processes* (Cambridge, MA: Harvard University Press, 2003), 229–241.

Table 4.2

Emotional Intelligence Scales

Scale	Sign	z-score with Success*	Statistical Significance**	Comment
Recognize own emotions	+	1.96	.06	Successful leaders have good awareness.
Recognize others' emotions	+	1.68	.09	Relationship to project success is obvious.
Regulating emotions	+	0.18	.86	This is the only EI scale that shows no relationship.
Social skills	+	1.78	.08	Key to effective teamwork.
Use emotions	+	1.12	.26	Directionally correct; some components are significant.
Optimism	+	2.0	.05	This is a measure of emotional strength in face of difficulties.

*The z-score, which is calculated from probit regressions, tells how far the coefficient for the particular variable is from a completely null result. A z-score of 1.96, for example, tells that the difference is nearly 2 standard errors away from being null. High z-scores are more statistically significant.
**The statistical significance is the probability that the result would appear randomly in repeated trials.

these scales relate to more and less successful complex project outcomes. The table confirms our common sense: effective leaders are adept with their emotions and in tune with the emotions of others.

The two scales with the strongest relationships to successful project results are recognition of one's own real-time emotions and optimism, closely followed by social skills. Only one of the scales has no discernible relationship with success: regulating one's emotions. Both the successful and unsuccessful leaders were quite strong on this measure, averaging four on the five-point measures that aggregate to this scale. This scale correlates very strongly (Pr.$|t| < .013$) with the Five-Factor-Model scale measuring neuroticism. As noted when we discussed that scale earlier, our group of project managers are fairly uniformly quite emotionally stable, a characteristic they share with engineers generally. This factor does not vary with project size or complexity. Therefore, there is very little meaningful variance for our analysis to pick up; indeed, this emotional intelligence scale displayed the least variance in our sample of all measures of personality and emotional intelligence.

Our conclusion then is that emotional intelligence plays an important role in fashioning the successful leader of complex projects. Significantly, our earlier study of project managerial success in smaller, simpler projects found that emotional intelligence did not play nearly as important a part in their success as it does for complex project leaders. This difference is not surprising. The project manager's job on smaller projects is often highly transactional. It is less about leadership and more about good management of tasks and assignments. By contrast, complex projects require both leadership and management. The leadership component is far more difficult and far more demanding of emotional and normal intelligence.

This raises an intriguing question: does the effective complex project leader also need to have been an effective project manager? In other words, could one have been rather unsuccessful as a manager of noncomplex projects, but a highly effective leader of complex projects? Perhaps surprisingly, we believe the answer is yes. The complex project leader does not (and probably should not) do project management as it is usually practiced. The role is to provide the vision of project success, generate and maintain alignment among all the stake-holders, and foster good communication between all of the subproject leaders and contractors.

THE APPROACH TO LEADERSHIP

As we discussed in Chapter 2, we fashioned a set of 12 leadership-related questions from Daniel Goleman's work. Three of those questions separate successful and unsuccessful complex project leaders quite clearly. The first question was, "I prefer to spend my time thinking about the project as a whole rather than its components." Almost all of the successful leaders agreed with that statement while about half of leaders of unsuccessful projects disagreed or were neutral. While this question would seem to be tapping the same qualities as the hedgehog/fox scale, the two items are actually not correlated.

Instead, we believe this question is tapping the project leaders who have genuinely graduated from the management of smaller projects to the leadership of megaprojects. The management of relatively simple projects is often about getting the details right, leaving no loose ends in the front-end, and executing with precision. All of those things are also critical for complex projects, but they are not the remit of the complex project director! Those things belong to the managers of the subprojects. The project leader's responsibility is above all the integration of the components into a successful asset.

The other two responses that were related to successful complex project leadership were:

1. When making decisions, I more often rely on the consensus-input of my project team than on my own experience and opinions.
2. As the project leader, I prefer not to delegate decision authority.

Successful project leaders strongly disagreed with the first statement and strongly agreed with the second. Unsuccessful leaders went the other way. Taken together, one might conclude that the successful complex project leadership style is dictatorial, but we believe this would be a profound misreading of the data. Recall that the successful project leaders are considerably more open than their unsuccessful counterparts. They are willing to listen to others' opinions, but they are unwilling to let others make *their* decisions. We are reminded of a wonderful story told about Abraham Lincoln. Lincoln was holding a meeting of his cabinet and called for a paper ballot vote on a course of action they had been debating. He tallied up the votes from slips of paper that cabinet members handed in and announced the result: "There are 12 ayes and one nay. The nay has it. Let's move on." On another question the successful leaders agreed with the statement, "I listen to the opinions of others even when I have pretty much already made up my mind." We don't find it surprising that the successful leaders do not attempt a consensus approach to decision making. The problem is not that consensus may be slow, although it is. The problem is that consensus implies that the leader will accept a decision she thinks is wrong in order to be a good sport. That's not leadership; that's being a good sport. It is often said that leadership is a lonely role. We suspect this is part of that observation.

One should not take from this discussion that good leaders want to make all of the decisions. On a complex project that will surely lead to the leader being overwhelmed with decisions that should be made by others. But they do want to make the decisions they believe need to be theirs and don't look for cover in having everyone agree. As we discuss how the selection of tasks and importance assigned to tasks differentiates the successful and unsuccessful leaders, we will see that those who like to micromanage the technical details tend to fail quite completely as complex project leaders. We will also see in Part II that the effective leaders focus on getting the best from those who work for them, which surely means letting those folks make the decisions that are appropriate to them. To do otherwise would surely lead to frustration on the part of the leader's reports. What we actually see is quite different: a burning desire to work for the effective leaders again on the next project. As a leader of leaders (the subproject managers) the effective leader will make the decisions that affect the whole project and leave virtually all of the decisions that affect any single part to the manager to which that part has been assigned.

THE EARLY CAREERS OF SUCCESSFUL LEADERS

Our typical project leader had been a project manager for about 12 years on average. More experienced leaders were a little more likely to have successful projects but the difference is far from statistically significant. When we control for other factors, such as full-functional representation on the owner team and the completeness of front-end definition, there isn't even a directional difference between more and less experienced project leaders. However, it is true that the more experienced project leaders have on average done a better job of the front-end work! (Pr. $|t| < .04$).

Very few of the leaders started their careers as project managers; that is a position one attains after a number of years in other roles in most cases. Most (74%) of the project leaders in our sample worked for the same company for their entire career. Those who started in another industry, however, were much more likely to be represented in the successful group.

Successful project leaders were over twice as likely to have started their career not just with another company, but in another industrial sector altogether. Again, we believe that is symptomatic of the successful leaders' openness and foxiness.

The more experienced project leaders were much more likely to have all critical owner functions on the team at the right time compared to less experienced directors (Pr.$|z| < .01$). Experienced leaders have learned, probably from bitter experience, that missing a function when developing a project can be devastating to project results. Each internal function, such as operations, or maintenance, or the commercial negotiator, or the environmental lead, is an internal stakeholder. When they are not present and involved, mistakes are made that will have to be corrected later at great expense. The more experienced project leader is also usually better at insisting that all functions involve themselves at the right time because she is more likely to have acquired some amount of moral authority over the course of her career. That moral authority makes it easier to twist arms as needed to get others to cooperate. The experienced leader is also more likely to have developed a network of friends and colleagues within the organization who can be called upon to help when a problem, such as not getting cooperation, is encountered. One of the fringe benefits of high emotional intelligence is more skill at network development.

What Types of Prior Experience Are Beneficial?

Figure 4.4 shows the prior work experiences within the company of the project leaders in our sample. The most common prior work experience listed was as a liaison to projects being run by another company of which their company was a joint venture partner. We call this NOV (nonoperated venture)

Figure 4.4
Prior Experience in Non–Project Leader Roles

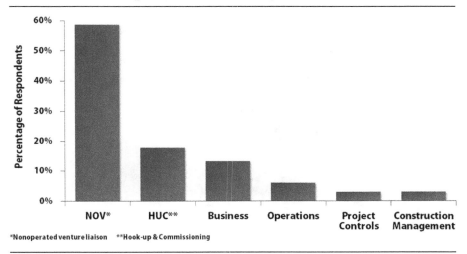

*Nonoperated venture liaison **Hook-up & Commissioning

experience. Some were formerly responsible for commissioning a prior project. About 14% had experience working in the
business side; a few had come from operations; and fewer still
had controls and construction management experience. Only
one type of prior company experience was strongly and posi-
tively associated with performance as a project leader: working
on an NOV.

NOV experience is one of the best predictors of project
leader success in our entire study. As shown in Figure 4.5,
over 70% of the successful project leaders had NOV experience versus 37% of the unsuccessful leaders. NOV experience,
however, appears to be a matter of happenstance rather than
design.

NOV experience is completely unrelated to any of the
other factors associated with successful leadership. But it
clearly has a powerfully beneficial effect. We theorize that
the NOV experience permits the aspiring complex project

Figure 4.5
Time Spent on Others' Projects Helps

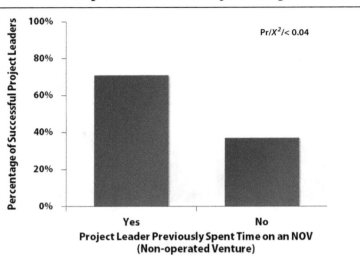

leader to do something very unusual: get paid to watch some-body else do the job they would rather do themselves. The NOV liaison is responsible for watching and reporting back to his own company how well the project to which he has been assigned is being run. The NOV liaison is a critic and the nature of the job requires that he think about what could be done better. We believe experience on an NOV should be a required part of the development process for aspiring megaproject leaders.

Unfortunately, the NOV liaison position is not highly val-ued in most companies. It is considered a fill-in assignment for project people who are between projects. As noted in Chapter 1, only about 15% of companies consider the rotation through the NOV liaison role as a developmental assignment. Yet it is a wonderful role for those open to learning. And being able to carry out the role well taps the soft skills that are essen-tial to leadership because without developing a relationship of trust with the project leader, who is employed by another company and almost surely a stranger, only the least possible information will be provided.[13]

Does Business Experience Help?

One of the surprises in our study was to find that prior experience in the business not only did not aid the project leader, it was actually associated with failure (Pr.$|z|$ < .024). The reason that those with business backgrounds did not fare well as project leaders is clear from the data: the group scored significantly lower on three of the six emotional intelligence scales and directionally lower in the other three.[14] We cannot know whether this is a fluke of the sample or represents an enduring relationship. But the implication is that those who have business backgrounds do not find projects a very comfortable home. That result may surprise no one in either the projects or business arena.

SUMMING UP: WHO ARE THESE SUCCESSFUL LEADERS?

In this chapter we have gotten to know who these successful leaders are through the prism of data. Even with such a cold lens, what comes through are a group of intelligent men and women who know themselves well and see others clearly. They are conscientious, just like the pool of engineers from

---

[13] We are indebted to our colleague, Katya Petrochenkov, who has studied nonoperated ventures extensively for these insights.

[14] In our sample those with a business background scored significantly lower on recognizing others' emotions (Pr. < .01), regulating their emotions (Pr. < .09), and using emotions (Pr. < .004). The scores on two other emotional intelligence (EI) scales – recognizing one's own emotions and optimism – were almost significant. All six EI scales had negative signs.

which they are drawn, but they are unusually open, open to the views and opinions of others, and open to different ways of approaching problems. In this important respect they differ from norms for engineers. They are generalists who thrive on working across many fronts and with people in many roles. But they often started their careers as very successful specialists. Their leadership styles are definitive but open. They come across as self-confident, but not arrogant. They are optimistic and somewhat extraverted, but also people who by their own words "like to reflect on things." These people do not all come from a single mold, but there are strong commonalities that should enable better and more systematic selection and development of complex project leaders in the future. In the next chapter we show how these personal traits translate into actions as project leaders.

CHAPTER 5

FROM PERSONALITY TO PRACTICE

In the last chapter we focused on the personality types and the sorts of emotional intelligence that are associated with more and less successful complex project leaders. In and of itself, however, that proves nothing. Personality and emotional intelligence don't do projects. People do projects by the way they behave. The only way the personality and emotional intelligence can have any effect on projects is if they induce, steer, or otherwise influence what leaders actually do day to day.

Superficially, there is very little that differentiates successful and unsuccessful leaders in our sample. Both groups are made up of mostly deeply experienced project professionals. Most had extensive formal training in how to do projects correctly. Almost all of the companies for which they work use very similar, stage-gated work processes. Nonetheless, we found in Chapter 4 that the successful leaders had rather different personalities from the unsuccessful and responded to the emotional intelligence scale survey in quite a different fashion. The connecting link is how personality and emotional intelligence affect leadership behaviors. Those behaviors in turn affect the level of cooperation and commitment that team members, internal stakeholders, and external stakeholders provide to the effort. Finally, what the leaders focus on and the cooperation they receive from others shape their ability to execute the practices that actually drive project outcomes.

Recall that in Chapter 3, very few of those involved in a major project actually work directly for the project leader. In a complex project, many hundreds of professionals and many thousands more blue-collar workers contribute to the project. No more than 15 to 30 of those professionals have their performance reviews written by the project leader. Therefore, to at least some extent, most have the option of not cooperating fully if they want to. While it is true that everyone has a boss, the boss may not be entirely on board with what the project is trying to do as well. An effective leader has to create an environment in which voluntary and whole-hearted cooperation is the norm, not the exception. It is simply impracticable for the project leader to have line-of-sight control over more than a tiny fraction of those contributing to the overall effort.

What we seek to establish in this chapter is illustrated by Figure 5.1.

Figure 5.1
Linking from Building Blocks to Outcomes

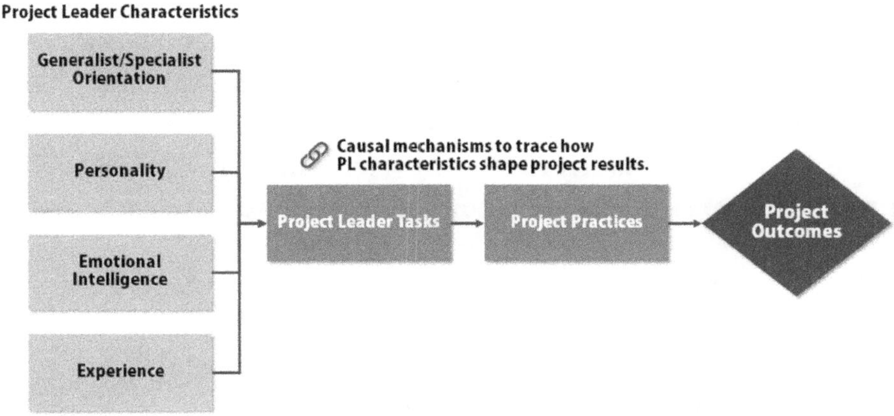

Project Leader Characteristics

- Generalist/Specialist Orientation
- Personality
- Emotional Intelligence
- Experience

Causal mechanisms to trace how PL characteristics shape project results.

Project Leader Tasks → Project Practices → Project Outcomes

In Chapter 4 we demonstrated the links between a generalist orientation, certain personality traits, especially openness, high emotional intelligence, and certain types of experience to more successful project results. Now we seek to trace through some of the causal mechanisms that get us from personal traits to project results by focusing on the actual tasks that project leaders think are important and how their decisions to focus on some tasks lead to degraded practices that in turn directly shape project results.

LEADER TASKS

My wife likes to say that, at the end of the day, people do what they really want to. Although (of course) I agree with that, I would add that I also believe people do what they are good at doing. Without even always being aware of it, they will steer their activities toward the things they do well and that give them greater satisfaction and away from things they find difficult and frustrating. I believe this is especially true of professionals, who are usually not closely monitored by supervisors. Keep this in mind as you read this section.

In our survey of project leaders, we asked them to list the tasks on which they personally spend the bulk of their time during a project. We also asked what tasks they considered most important and which they considered least valuable, even if necessary. These questions were open-ended so the respondents could list whatever tasks they wished. The tasks that the project leaders listed most often fell into these nine categories:

1. Stakeholder management.
2. Communication.
3. Project work process.
4. People management.
5. Project controls (cost and schedule).

6. Contractors and   8. Engineering (and other
   vendors.   technical tasks).
7. Project management.   9. Construction safety.

These nine tasks covered almost all of the task–related responses by our project leaders surveyed.

In Table 5.1 we explore the differences between successful and unsuccessful project leaders in how important they believe the tasks are to success and how much time they spend on the tasks.

Referring to the table, there is no difference in how much time the two groups of project leaders spend in stakeholder management. But there is a substantial difference in how they see it. The successful group views stakeholder management as important and valuable as well as necessary. The unsuccessful project leaders tend to see it as only necessary. We believe

Table 5.1

Leaders' Views of Tasks

Task Category	Leaders That Consider Task to Be Important	Leaders That Spend More Time on Task
Stakeholder Management	Successful Leaders	*No difference*
Project Work Process	Unsuccessful Leaders	Unsuccessful Leaders
Project Controls *(cost and schedule)*	Unsuccessful Leaders	Unsuccessful Leaders
Project Management	*No difference*	*No difference*
Communication	Successful Leaders	*No difference*
People Management	Successful Leaders	Successful Leaders
Contractors and Vendors	Successful Leaders	Successful Leaders
Engineering *(and other technical tasks)*	Unsuccessful Leaders	Unsuccessful Leaders
Construction Safety	*No difference*	*No difference*

the reason that there is no difference in time spent is that stakeholder management is generally nondiscretionary. When your management shows up for their quarterly review with the joint venture partners and the government in tow, opting out is not a choice, even if it is viewed as wasteful work.

The unsuccessful project leaders view the work process and controls as much more important than the successful leaders and they spend more of their time on those activities. Work process refers to making sure that deliverables meet gate-inspection requirements and that work is being done in accordance with company procedures. This activity is generally the work of the subproject managers on complex projects and not the work of the leader. Project controls refers to monitoring contractor hours and productivity, reviewing progress reports, and the like. The typical complex project has a whole organization devoted to controls. While we would expect the project leader to be concerned about controls, we would not expect it to be a significant consumer of their time. Unsuccessful project leaders disagree.

Unsuccessful leaders reported spending more time on engineering and other technical tasks and viewing their doing of those tasks as more important than the successful leaders. These tasks are indeed critical to generating successful projects. But that is not the issue. The issue is should the project leader be devoting time and energy to those tasks and the answer is *no*. Interestingly, years of experience makes no difference in the mix of tasks that project leaders see as important with the exception of contracting.

The successful leaders place much more value on communication and people management than their less successful colleagues. They see these tasks as central to their success. They also spend more time and place more emphasis on dealing with contractors and other suppliers. Contractors are critical to these projects as they do almost all of the detailed engineering and construction and fabrication work. A vendor who is late with a piece of equipment can disrupt the entire project. Especially on large complex projects, the relationships with contractors have to be more as partners and less as superior to subordinate. A transactional approach doesn't work well with contractors on complex projects because the owner's team cannot closely monitor all, or even most, of the work that the contractors are doing. Therefore, the contractors and critical vendors must be communicated with so that mutual trust can be developed. Building trust, a critical leadership skill and activity, reduces the need for close supervision.

No difference is reported in time spent on safety and its importance between successful and less successful leaders. And the answers to safety questions were unrelated to personality or the emotional intelligence scales. This is not surprising in the slightest. Because construction is inherently a dangerous occupation, a focus on safety is so deeply ingrained and politically correct among project management professionals that everyone answered the same way. To suggest that safety is unimportant or that one spends little time on it is simply not done in the project management community.

The overall picture that emerges is that successful leaders spend their time and energy on the soft side of project leadership while the unsuccessful spend more of their time on the technical, procedural, and transactional side of the ledger. The data clearly show that those who work that soft side are much more likely to have more successful projects. So, what is it about their emotional and personality makeup that leads them to work the people side harder while delegating the more technical work to others?

We believe that Table 5.2 largely answers the question of the relationship between personality and emotional intelligence

Table 5.2

Tasks Project Leaders Spend More Time On

	Work Process	Project Controls	Project Management	Communication	People Management	Engineering	Contracting
Big 5 Personality Scales							
Openness	—				+		
Conscientious			—	+	+		+
Extravert				—*	+		+
Agreeable							
Neurotic			+				—
Emotional Intelligence Scales							
Recognize Own Emotions			—		+		
Recognize Others' Emotions			—		+		
Regulate Emotions			—		+		+
Social Skills		—	—		+		
Use Emotions	—	—			+		+
Optimism		—			+		+

*One of our reviewers, a psychologist by training, speculates that this result may be an artifact of how extraverts and introverts would answer this question. Extraverts communicate more often by nature and may not think they spend much time on it because they are not spending more time communicating at work than they do in other aspects of their daily life. By contrast, the introvert may be more acutely aware of the time and effort devoted to communication because it doesn't come as easily.

and successful complex project leadership. The time spent and the importance attached to every task is substantially shaped by the personality and emotional makeup of the leader. In the table a plus sign (+) means that those scoring higher on the personality or emotional intelligence index spent more time on a particular task. A minus sign (–) indicates those scoring lower on that measure of personality or emotional intelligence spent more time on a task. All of the cells with a plus or minus are showing a statistically significant result. Many of the relationships are significant at one chance in a hundred or less.

Of the 28 statistically significant relationships shown in the table, only one has a sign contrary to our hypothesis: we did not expect the negative relationship between extraversion and less time reported spent on communication. We believe that is a fluke of the way the question was approached. The other 27 statistically significant relationships are as hypothesized. The blank cells indicate that the relationships did not meet the threshold for statistical significance. However, all those that approached significance (t-ratio > 1.5) are in the expected direction. Many of the relationships are significant at one chance in a hundred and a few at one chance in a thousand. The strength of the relationships is quite remarkable given the small sample and reinforces the finding that personality and emotional intelligence shape project leadership behavior.

So, what do all these relationships tell us? Leaders who are more open and with systematically higher emotional intelligence spend their time on communication and people management. Those who score lower on emotional intelligence spend their time on work process, controls, and project management. In other words, those who are more adept with dealing with people, spend more time dealing with people. Not a very surprising result! But a very important one because the management of complex projects is all about leadership rather than management, and leadership is inevitably all about people.

Those who spend more time working with contracts are an interesting lot. They are conscientious, which means they do things from a sense of duty and propriety. They are also optimistic extraverts who score low on neuroticism, so they are a hearty group emotionally. Also note they are good at using emotions and are strong in regulating their emotions. Both of those traits are excellent in negotiating situations, which is the normal situation in the owner/contractor relationship. Those who are more neurotic (emotionally unstable) avoid dealing with the contractors. This really isn't surprising. Dealing with contractors is often the most emotionally taxing thing that a project leader does. The owner/contractor relationship is often fraught with a great deal of conflict as owner and contractor objectives are always to some extent at odds. Dealing with conflict takes a toll on everyone but an especially high toll on those who are more neurotic. Those who considered contracting important were also very likely (80% of them) to have had experience as a liaison in a joint venture, while less than half of those not considering the area important had such experience $(\text{Pr.} \,|\, X^2 \,| < .05)$. They also had more years of experience as a complex project leader $(\text{Pr.} \,|\, t \,| < .05)$. Willingness to work with contractors without being a pushover may be an important selection criterion for complex project leadership.

When we consider personality, emotional intelligence, and tasks given priority, two models of complex project leaders emerge: *the holistic leader* and *the downward-focused leader*. The holistic leader focuses attention upward and outward toward stakeholders, contractors, and vendors while focusing downward attention on management of people and communicating with all involved. The downward-focused leader appears to be trying to manage a complex project in the same manner as a simple project. His focus is on the actual work of the project rather than the leadership of the effort. He therefore focuses on getting the work process and procedures correct, the engineering work done, and the controls prepared. The irony of the downward-focused leader is that focusing on getting the work done rather than on the cast of characters results in the work not getting done. We will see this immediately below as the holistic leader is able, working through others, to get the key practices completed while the downward-focused leader cannot.

The project leaders who fail to manage up and out as well as down are trying to run a complex megaproject as if it was a simpler, easier project. They never really graduated to the premier league. But the critical thing to understand is that their personalities and emotional makeup always made that graduation unlikely. Most importantly, the traits of the holistic leader versus the downward-focused leader are knowable *ex ante*.

LEADER PERSONALITY, LEADER TASKS, AND KEY PROJECT PRACTICES

There are six project practices, illustrated in Figure 5.2, that are essential to project success for projects large and small, simple and complex. If a project leader is going to make a difference, the difference will show up in how these six practices are implemented on a project. As suggested in the illustration, the practices flow one from another and carry a certain degree of necessary sequentiality. The more complex a project becomes, the more difficult these practices are to do successfully. For example, the objectives of simple projects are

Figure 5.2
Six Core Practices for Project Success

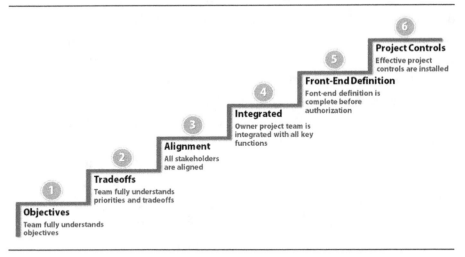

usually quite straightforward. The objectives of a complex project tend to be larger in number and more difficult to reconcile one to another. Furthermore, objectives in complex projects frequently trade off against each other and can even conflict. For example, the objectives of lowest cost and best environmental footprint are usually impossible to fully reconcile and so must be balanced instead. The communication of how to do that must be nuanced and well communicated or the project team will be thoroughly confused. Complex projects typically have more stakeholders in the form of joint venture partners, government permitting authorities, local communities, and nongovernmental organizations (NGOs). All major petroleum developments also have a host of internal stakeholders as well. Indeed, every practice is more difficult on complex projects because there is so much more work to get accomplished, rarely enough time, and too many cooks vying to get into the kitchen. So, let's trace through how project leader traits and what project leaders consider the important tasks for themselves affect these six key practices.

Clarity of Objectives and Tradeoffs

Every project starts with objectives and the clarity of the objectives weighs heavily on all project outcomes. The business sponsor whose project is being developed and executed should create the objectives of the project. But it is the task of the project leader to articulate those objectives to the subproject teams and their managers. When we performed evaluations of the projects executed by the complex project leaders in our sample, we asked the owner team to rate the clarity of the project's objectives and how well they understood the priorities on the projects and how those priorities should be traded off to produce the desired outcome. For example, cost and schedule always trade off at some point and the team's understanding of how they should trade cost for schedule or schedule for cost informs their decision making. Clarity of objectives is highly related to three of the emotional intelligence scales:

- Understanding the emotions of others (Pr. < .035).
- Social skills (Pr. < 0.05).
- Ability to use emotions (Pr. < 0.04).

These relationships are not surprising because these emotional intelligence measures are indicators of the leader's ability to communicate effectively and forcefully.

The team's understanding of the priorities and tradeoffs among priorities is where most of the difficulty arises. The objectives may be clear, but exactly how the various objectives should be managed vis-à-vis each other is often hazy.

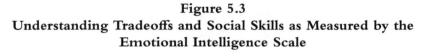

Figure 5.3

Understanding Tradeoffs and Social Skills as Measured by the Emotional Intelligence Scale

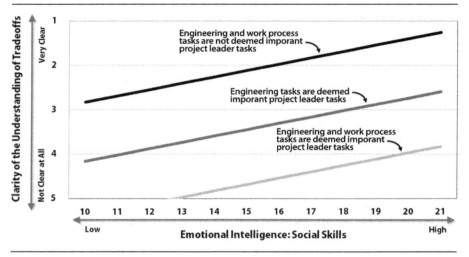

Emotional intelligence measures correlate with an understanding of tradeoffs even more strongly than with objectives:

- Understanding the emotions of others (Pr. < 0.01).
- Social skills (Pr. < .004).
- Ability to use emotions (Pr. < 0.02).

And for the understanding of tradeoffs, we see the project leaders' view of what is important to focus on also comes into play. Figure 5.3 displays the understanding of tradeoffs and social skills as measured by the Emotional Intelligence Scale. When the leader has high emotional intelligence and is not prioritizing engineering and work process tasks for himself, he is making the tradeoffs crystal clear to the team. When the leader's focus is on engineering tasks, the clarity declines significantly, and if the leader also prioritizes work process tasks, the tradeoffs are not clear at all. This merely demonstrates an obvious point: when the project leader focuses on work that is not core to leadership, the key leadership tasks suffer.

Stakeholder Management

Unfortunately, when most of these projects were evaluated, we did not have a measure for quality of stakeholder alignment. We do know, however, that project leaders who considered stakeholder alignment important and spent more of their time doing it scored significantly higher in emotional intelligence. This relationship is not surprising. Managing stakeholders calls for negotiating and diplomatic skills. Those who are better at recognizing others' emotions (Pr. $< .023$), quickly identifying their own emotions (Pr. $< .01$), and regulating their emotions (Pr. $< .01$) will find stakeholder alignment tasks easier and therefore spend more time doing them.

Owner–Team Integration

An owner team is integrated when all of the needed owner functions are incorporated into the project team during scope development. Three requirements must also be met: the members of the team must be empowered to make decisions on behalf of their function, a reasonable degree of continuity of people is required, and the team members report to the project leader, not back to their functional managers. Owner-team integration is essential because without it information that is vital to the development of the right scope is likely to be missing, incorrect, or not timely. That in turn makes front-end definition ineffective and generates project-killing changes during execution. Owner-team integration improves results on all projects, but it is especially important on complex projects because complex projects are much more heavily damaged by late changes than simpler projects. When owner

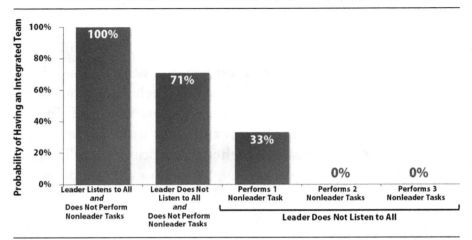

Figure 5.4
Effective Leaders Listen and Don't Do Others' Work

teams do not include all relevant functions during development, the chances that the project will unravel during execution increase significantly.[1]

Project leaders do not have unilateral control over team integration. But as Figure 5.4 makes clear, project leaders do have considerable influence over whether all functions are represented on the team. Figure 5.4 shows that two types of factors are at work. First, when project leaders answered the question "I always listen to others even if I have mostly made up my mind" affirmatively, they were much more likely to have everyone on board. The causality between being a good listener and team integration cannot be proven, but one can easily imagine that good listeners make joining a team much more appealing.

---

[1] For a discussion of the importance of integrated owner teams on complex projects, see Edward Merrow, *Industrial Megaprojects* (Hoboken, NJ: Wiley, 2011): 168 ff.

The other factor that plays in team integration is whether the project leader really prefers to do other peoples' work.[2] Project leaders who believed that focusing on work process, engineering tasks, or controls was their work were much less likely to have integrated teams. Those that put any one of those items as important for a project leader had the chances of integrating the team fall by a third. Those that put two or more as important tasks for themselves had almost no chance of having an integrated team. Again, imagining the causal path is not difficult, who wants to be on a team where the boss wants to do your job? That is a recipe for the situation no professional likes – being micromanaged. Project leaders who focus on these technical tasks are managing downward rather than holistically. That's what project managers do on smaller, less complex projects. But on the projects in our set, managing downward leads to failure. Most of the action is out and up.

Front–End Loading (FEL)

The fifth key practice is front-end loading (FEL). Downward-focused project leaders produced projects with much poorer FEL ($Pr. |t| < .006$) than project leaders who focused on the project more holistically. This relationship is only for projects for which there was no turnover in the project leadership position from FEL forward through execution so the project

---

[2] When project leaders completed the survey that included their task preferences, the answers were not provided with respect to any particular project. The project leaders were not informed as to which of their projects we would include in our sample and we asked them to respond generally and not with respect to any particular project. So when they answer, for example, that they believe engineering tasks are important for them to do and they focus a good deal of their time there, it is not because the last project had engineering problems. It is because they believe that is where they should focus.

Figure 5.5
Factors Driving Front-End Loading

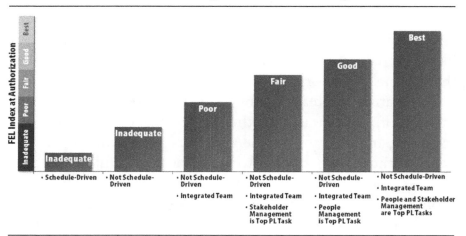

leader who answered our survey was leading the project during front-end loading.

Figure 5.5 shows how various factors drive the completeness of the front-end work on our projects. If the project is schedule-driven and no other factors are at work, the FEL is grossly inadequate and the failure of the project is virtually assured. If the team is integrated and the project is not schedule-driven the average FEL score improves very substantially (Pr. | t | < .03). If the project leader gives high priority to stakeholder management, the FEL improves still more (Pr. | t | < .02). If the project leader gives weight to people management, the FEL improves to "good" and for the first time the project has better than a 50/50 chance to succeed (Pr. | t | < .001). *Giving priority to people management was the single most important factor in improving FEL.* If the project leader gives priority to both stakeholder management and people management, the FEL score achieved averages "best practical" and the success of the project is now very likely.

The causality of the factors cited above is straightforward. When projects are schedule-driven, FEL is routinely short-changed in the name of speed.[3] That is why schedule-driven megaprojects are almost always failures.[4] Team integration is necessary to getting the scope of a project right. When a function (e.g., operations) is missing during FEL, their needed viewpoint is not represented and FEL quality suffers. Misalignment of stakeholders is one of the most common problems in getting front-end loading done well in projects. Sometimes partners simply do not want to pay for the front-end work. Sometimes permitting authorities change their minds about requirements, which translates into the front-end work being incorrect. Sometimes an NGO successfully pushes for a change late in FEL. Finally, the most important driver of better FEL is a focus on people management by the project leader. Front-end loading in a complex project is difficult to organize and keep organized. A lot of work is going on in parallel and often at a number of locations around the world, which makes accommodating changes very challenging. There are lots of late nights and long weekends of work. If team members burn out before the work is done, FEL suffers. The focus on people management helps ensure that doesn't happen.

Project Controls

The final practice needed to help ensure project success is the installation of strong project controls. At IPA we measure project controls with an index composed of degree of owner involvement, the use of extensive physical progressing, and the

---

[3] Speed is not actually achieved, however. On average, schedule-driven projects end up taking so much longer in execution due to changes that any time saved in FEL is lost, along with a lot of money.
[4] Merrow, *Industrial Megaprojects*, 309–321.

use of frequent and systematic reporting from those executing the project back to the owner. Four factors are found to drive the controls index in our sample of complex projects:

- The completeness of front-end loading (Pr.|t| < .001)
- Understanding of project objectives (Pr.|t| < .001)
- Problems aligning joint venture partners (Pr.|t| < .002)
- The validation of the authorization estimate by the owner (Pr.|t| < .02).

The four factors above account for nearly three-quarters ($R^2 = 0.74$) of the variation in controls practices in our sample. The first three are, of course, factors we have already discussed above and the last is simply common sense. The most important single factor is front-end loading. A poorly defined project cannot be effectively controlled. Without good FEL the quantities of materials that will be engineered and installed cannot be measured. Without a baseline of quantities, progress is impossible to measure accurately. Clarity of project objectives figures in controls because unclear objectives are a source of change. If a project suffers enough changes, controls begin to fall apart because the baseline becomes meaningless. Problems with joint-venture partners are an *ex post* measure, but reflect a failure in the stakeholder-alignment process. Failures in stakeholder alignment lead not only to changes but to delays, especially delays around funding at authorization. Such delays erode the quality of the project's baseline as market prices and availabilities change. Finally, estimate validation ensures that the baseline for assessing progress is firm and has not been manipulated by the organization, usually a contractor, making the estimate.

The six practices build one upon another. But underpinning getting the practices in place and executed properly is a holistic leader who understands that people, rather than process, actually do projects.

PERSONALITY, EMOTIONAL INTELLIGENCE, AND LEADERSHIP STYLES

The behavior of project leaders may be shaped somewhat by skills and training, but it is clearly modulated through personality and emotional intelligence. Those with more closed personalities and lower emotional intelligence tend to emphasize work process and technical tasks and shun the people-to-people tasks. That is just natural. But the people tasks are what generate success, especially in the complex projects where transactional management cannot work.

These findings also help us understand why the manner in which complex project leaders are selected is not working. The selections are usually based on how well the person has performed as a manager on smaller and less complex projects. They may be given training in people-management skills but the effectiveness of such training is rarely tested and may not be effective in any case. Personality traits are considered by psychologists to be very stable and therefore not easily influenced by training. Whether emotional intelligence can be improved with training in adults is very much an open debate. How one comes down on the issue of whether emotional intelligence can be trained is a very important consideration for how the project leader development and selection process should work.

We have examples of project leaders who were highly transactional and even harsh as young project managers but decided at some point in their career to change their management approach completely to do a better job of managing people. What we do not know is whether they always had a high degree of emotional intelligence but elected not to manage projects with it or whether that emotional intelligence was acquired over time.

So, should we conclude from this discussion that these project leaders are a group of nice warm, soft-hearted folks who have really good soft skills and not much else? That would be a profound misreading of the data. The successful project leaders generally started their careers as strong technical professionals who excelled at their work. These are people who feel comfortable in a position of authority and reject consensus decision making – groupthink – categorically. They dislike delegating their decisions to others and will drive to meet project objectives even if it stretches and stresses their teams and themselves. But these are also people who have come to understand, in the words of Joseph Brewer (whom we will meet in the next chapter), that "The hard stuff is easy; it's the soft stuff that's hard."

SUMMARY OF PART I

Figure 5.6 summarizes what we have learned and established in Part I and prepares for our discussions with successful leaders in Part II.

The successful project leaders of complex projects we found to have generalist orientations in our hedgehog/fox scale and unusually open personalities as measured by the Five-Factor Model. They were also found to be emotionally stable and highly conscientious. They were also considerably more emotionally intelligent than their less successful counterparts. These traits when combined with good learning experiences – experience in other industries and/or experience working on a joint venture in a liaison role – provided the platform on which their project leadership careers were built.

Figure 5.6
Summarizing Part I

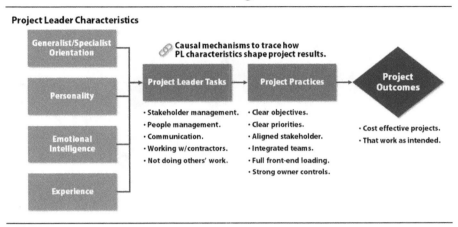

We next established that their personalities and emotional intelligence made it easier and more likely for them to embrace and practice tasks that are central to leadership: keeping everyone aligned and moving forward and dealing with those outside their immediate line control effectively. We also found that leaders who focused on technical and procedural work tended to fail. Finally, we traced through how the choice of tasks and importance attached to them affected the ability of the project to implement six key practices that ultimately drive project success.

PART TWO

In Part II, we describe the journeys and approaches to complex project leadership of seven extraordinary people. Although each person is unique in many ways, there are also many ways these seven people are alike. They come from different types of companies, sometimes in different industries, and from different countries and cultures. But their approaches to leadership seem very much the same. We end this part by suggesting an improved process for selecting and developing complex project leaders.

CHAPTER 6

JOSEPH BREWER

Encouragement + Alignment = A Passionate Team

Joseph Brewer was most recently the chief implementation officer (a joint project leader) of one of the most complex process projects ever undertaken. The project developed, designed, and constructed over two dozen integrated chemical plants in a single project. More than 40 contractors were involved with a construction workforce exceeding 55,000 at peak. The fact that the project was completed successfully refutes those who claim that "sometimes projects are just too difficult to do well."[1]

We asked Joseph for his views on what makes a successful project leader on such large and complex endeavors. "Well, you can't really talk about project leadership without first talking about what makes good leaders," was how Joseph started his response. He then went on to list and discuss the requirements he believes are needed for successful project leaders. It's all about how leaders conduct themselves. Here is Joseph's list of behaviors and attributes that successful project leaders demonstrate:

- Leaders are facilitative.
- Leaders are encouragers.

---

[1] For a wonderful narrative on this remarkable project and how it was led, see Joseph C. Brewer, Jr., *When Mega Goes Giga: The Rocket Ride on Dow and Aramco's Record-Setting Petrochemical Project,* forthcoming.

- Leaders say "thank you" a lot and mean it.
- Leaders take corrective actions.
- Leaders insist on alignment.
- Leaders are inspirational.

It was obvious from the ease of his answer that Joseph had considered the subject a great deal and was perfectly comfortable in his response. One of the most interesting aspects of this discussion was the tie Joseph made between saying "thank you" (and meaning it) and the ability to correct team members and others when they were straying from alignment on critical issues. He said the more you say "thank you," the more effective correction becomes. Of course, this is the sort of leader that would tend to score higher on the Emotional Intelligence Scale discussed in Chapters 4 and 5. The behaviors listed above engender the loyalty and trust that facilitates developing a network of trusted professionals who are always willing to be on the leader's team and willing to move mountains until the project is delivered successfully.

We asked Joseph's supervisor who gave him responsibility for his first megaproject why he selected Joseph from a number of strong candidates to lead the effort. He replied:

Joseph has many great attributes that became apparent over the time he worked for me. He has the ability to visualize the multiple steps needed to achieve something and to keep them in control during the normal chaos. That and an exceptional understanding of the supply chain dynamics of projects make it possible for him to frame a project effectively. Most important, he has great judgment for people and how their talents can fit into a team. His demeanor combines cool-headedness,[2]

---

[2] High on the regulating emotion scale from Emotional Intelligence Scale (EIS).

good humor,[3] and tenacity,[4] key ingredients for a good project leader.

It was significant for us that Joseph listed alignment as one of the core tasks of any complex project leader. Lack of alignment is a chief reason for project failure. Complex projects are a collection of internal and external stakeholders pursuing a common goal while also pursuing different goals as well. As Joseph said, "Joint ventures in the Middle East taught me the critical importance of alignment and I saw firsthand that people and teams can achieve amazing things when alignment is achieved." It is then incredibly unhelpful (and daft) when management actively works to create misalignment by developing functional KPIs that are at odds with project success. When the project leader relentlessly pursues alignment, he becomes the glue that binds the entire effort together. He facilitates everyone keeping their organization's goals, which can often conflict with project success, sufficiently subdued to permit forward progress.

Joseph grew up in a refinery town in southeast Texas. When he was five years old, he got his first tour of the oil refinery where his grandfather and father worked. Joseph graduated from college with a degree in electrical engineering and naturally went to work in the same refinery where his father and grandfather had worked. He joined the refinery as an operations engineer with a focus on helping the refinery move from automation driven by pneumatic controls (a mechanical discipline) to automation driven by electronic controls (an electrical discipline). However, within a few years, Joseph said, "I could see to the end of my life there" and couldn't imagine

---

[3] High on the optimism scale from the EIS.
[4] High on the conscientiousness scale from the Five-Factor Model.

doing the same thing in the same place forever. A common trait we observed in all the successful leaders was an itch to try something else to expand and diversify their horizons. We suspect that one characteristic of good project leaders is that they are easily bored by repetitive tasks and that such people are drawn to project work because projects offer a constantly changing work front.

As we established in Chapter 4, all our leaders are engineers by background and engineers tend to be specialists – hedge-hogs, if you prefer. Yet our successful leaders are foxes and this desire to constantly seek more, expand the boundaries of their knowledge, and learn new skills and domains fits nicely with a foxy personality. Joseph credits the moment when he recognized the need to seek something else outside the town in which he grew up as the first pivot point that would eventually lead him to project management. After talking with several friends who were neither connected to nor resident in his hometown, Joseph applied for and got a job with his current employer in Houston.

Expecting to stay only for three years or so in the new company, Joseph joined a leading global company in the chemicals sector. Given his background as an electrical engi-neer, he started by working on power plants. After building a few geothermal power plants in Southern California and spending the 1980s gaining experience as a lead electrical engineer and then as an assistant project manager, Joseph real-ized that he had learned all he could as the lead in a technical area. That was the second pivotal moment in his early career.

It is critically important to point out that although our suc-cessful leaders are foxy or more generalist, every one of them *first* worked his or her way up to achieve the highest level of competence in their respective domain. Despite being foxes, they were very good engineers! In working with many of

our clients in the past decade, we often encounter smart professionals responsible for megaprojects who did not get the
opportunities to achieve top level of expertise in their domains
primarily because there were more projects than project directors and leaders,[5] which meant far too quick movement from
project to project, but also because deep, specialist, domain
technical competence wasn't seen as a precursor for project
management leadership roles. Technical domain expertise and
project management expertise are often viewed as two independent domains. What is common for our strongest project
leaders is that they were successful in their specialty that started
their careers, but were always looking for something larger, not
in the sense of higher status, but in the sense of broader and
more holistic than their initial specialty.

Joseph wanted to expand his horizons and test his skills in
running organizations and managing people – and not just
end his career as a subject matter expert. Without much organizational support for the change he sought, Joseph spent two
additional years in the same domain expert role, becoming
more frustrated. This frustration culminated in a Friday afternoon, after-work whining session with an older fellow project
engineer, one of his mentors, who woke Joseph's passion by
confronting him; "Joseph, you are either going to have to shut
up or do something about it."

Working through the day and studying at night, Joseph
obtained an MBA that stirred and reoriented his thinking. The
business education provided him with a vista of how commercial, marketing, finance, and business functions think without
making him want to become a businessman. After earning

---

[5] In the contemporary oil industry landscape, this problem will actually be exacerbated
as many organizations have "optimized their human capital" (a euphemism for layoffs)
and so a significant number of professionals have left the industry.

his MBA, he finally got a supervisory role in the electrical engineering function. The supervisory role was followed by a two-year stint as the division manager supporting small manufacturing sites that eventually merged into one large division of all the small manufacturing sites in the United States. Joseph's new position for another two-year stint was as head of engineering and maintenance. As Joseph puts it, "In [this company], the beaten path is major manufacturing sites and small manufacturing sites are 'off the beaten path.' But I was happy because there were great leaders with a great set of talents hidden in these small sites." It also gave him a lot more freedom to explore doing things his way.

As Joseph reflected on his career, he said, "It was probably when I moved to Ohio to become the Eastern Division engineering manager that I first began the transition to being what you call a leader of leaders. All of my subsequent assignments were leader of leaders' roles – and thus were preparatory for my project director assignments on the Kuwait and Saudi megaprojects." We believe this is very important because what distinguishes the successful project leaders from those who failed is that the former made that pivot into being a leader of leaders while the latter did not. Without that change, one will continue to apply project *management* principles to a project *leadership* role.

After this stint as disciplinary chief of engineering and maintenance, Joseph was invited to serve as the project manager for a joint venture with complex commercial arrangements that not only involved two American private companies, including his organization, but also a European Union (EU) government entity for a power plant in one of the EU countries.

How he was selected for the project manager position on the power project is a story in itself. Joseph's company and the power company had worked together on a project in the States: "The working relationships and team dynamics were absolutely horrible, with yelling and screaming and all sorts of histrionics. It was so bad they brought in an industrial psychologist to listen and try to counsel the teams. So, when the EU project came along they called on me because I had a reputation of knowing how to get along with folks, and how to get team members to get along. That was the start of my project management education."

As most readers can imagine from their own experience, such a complex context with several shaping issues is bound to lead to challenges and of course this one did. Due to the sale of the project midstream by the principal owner, the project ended up in a dispute with the new owners and Joseph spent four years in arbitration after the execution of the project, in addition to his full-time job responsibilities. We believe that was the crucible that forged one of the most successful leaders for complex projects. As Joseph himself attests, "I am pretty good relationally, but this was my baptism that some people can be really tough to deal with." He describes the arbitration as an important teachable moment: "I learned an immense amount about contracts, claims, litigation, arbitration, and professional expert witnesses," in the EPC (engineering, procurement, and construction) industry. This knowledge that Joseph gained and used successfully throughout his career about human behavior and supply chain issues, including contracts, is what the manager who gave Joseph his first complex project was referring to. That is part of the supply chain understanding cited by his manager above.

We are reminded of an anecdote that an ex-army ranger once told us. Building upon his experiences on frontlines of war, he started a firm that helps executives find ways to transfer leadership experiences to junior colleagues, quickly, efficiently, and through the power of storytelling. In doing so, he interviews leaders in an industrial sector to understand the leadership experiences that are considered critical along the journey. One such experience relayed to him by hospital administrators is about litigation. As the hospital administrators put it to him, "You can be the best surgeon and best doctor with tremendous credentials. But you are not really a practicing doctor until you have to emotionally deal with the family of a patient who dies under your care or unless you have been sued at least once." Although this may sound morbid and even coarse, it is true that some experiences bring about the true reality of the job. Similarly, we believe that arbitration claims are real experiences in capital projects that are critical to the development of a leader. That of course does not mean that leaders should look for such opportunities, but it does mean that deliberately exposing future leaders to complex and difficult situations early in their careers can provide a critical stepping-stone.

With the successful completion of the power project in Europe, Joseph returned to his home office to manage the projects department, the project leadership segment of the larger engineering and construction organization of his owner chemical company. In this role, he was also a key leader overseeing the ownership, maintenance, and continuous improvement of the company's common projects process. After this stint overseeing the execution of large projects, Joseph got the opportunity to frame and then implement a complex $4 billion petrochemical plant expansion in the Middle East. That was the beginning of his 15-year run as a project director of large complex joint venture (JVs) capital investments. These projects were delivered successfully, including a $16 billion project that was delivered as one of the most cost-effective megaprojects ever executed. That project capped his

41-year journey in the project management and engineering profession.

Hopefully, this detailed account of a successful project leader's journey provides the readers, and more importantly, those responsible for finding and nurturing the future leaders in their organizations, the message that the path from an incoming engineering graduate to future leader of complex projects isn't linear. In fact, it might necessarily have to be a bit tortuous so that the future leader is exposed to a variety of experiences that each build upon the person's foundational skills.

Of course, a professional journey as described above is only helpful if the person is receptive to such exposure. In other words, there are some inherent characteristics that a person must have, as discussed in Chapter 4, for such exposure to have a maximal impact. Joseph exemplifies such qualities. Having come to know Joseph over the last 15 years of his professional life, I think the most important single quality that draws people to him as a leader is a complete lack of arrogance. I was going to say humility but that might be interpreted as weak, which would draw a good laugh from those who know him well. But Joseph never feels the need to make himself seem better by putting someone else down.

In addition to some innate qualities and deliberately curated career trajectories, as we will see in all the leadership profiles, what's also important for successful leadership development is lots of good mentors. It is no exception in the case of Joseph, who says he received mentoring from "… a very diverse set of people at different times in life and at different places … these mentors were not official mentors [that the company] appointed. These were all inadvertent mentors. People who you learn to trust by just working with them. You build a relationship with them." That is a critical point and maybe a reason why official corporate mentorship programs are not very effective. We heard from several leaders that their best mentors were people in a job that wasn't like the one they were in. The key was trust established through working together and a mentee who was open to learning from others. One of the themes that developed in our interviews with successful project leaders is they all had mentors who they sought out and never the mentors who were designated for them.

The openness to building trust and learning from others is the key to Joseph's success. As he describes it, Joseph's plumb line is the learnings about best practices the industry is currently following (or at least should be following) or the mistakes that others are currently making and that he is constantly collecting either through peer reviews, external reviews, or fresh-eye reviews. In fact, Joseph's belief is that "megaprojects should have at least one fresh-eye review per year [whether the process calls for it or not]." Joseph strikes us as very methodical in the way he constructed lessons over the course of his career. One of the authors participated with Joseph recently on a fresh-eyes review team of a project experiencing difficulty. As we talked with members of that project, Joseph not only could cite the right practice that could have been followed, he could explain why the practice worked, and recite the data as well as his own experience that supported that the practice works.

Joseph is unlike the other project leaders we interviewed in an instructive way: he spent most of his career outside project management. His first project leadership assignment was a large and potentially fractious joint venture because he had the emotional intelligence skills needed. His next two project assignments were to very large megaprojects in the Middle East. The rest of his career was spent in various disciplinary managerial roles in the engineering organization of

Dow Chemical Company. This suggests that leadership skills and temperament are more important to the complex project leader role than project management experience.

In addition to openness, trust is engendered by Joseph through the behaviors discussed in Chapter 5 that link with high emotional intelligence. Joseph's success in this regard is manifest through the consistency of the people who have worked for him on his three-project management career. In fact, there are four to six people who have chosen to work with and for Joseph on multiple endeavors over the past 15 years. Their loyalty to the project leader for over a decade is built on a foundation of mutual respect based on shared growth, shared experiences, and shared learnings. Joseph achieves this by being inspirational, creating a sense of building something that you will be proud to be a part of, being the chief encourager, and spending a disproportionate time on seeking alignment with everyone. As he put it, "Encouragement + Alignment = Passion" and clearly he has achieved that for the people who followed him on multiple projects. This is a true hallmark of leadership that we will see repeated in other profiles.

CHAPTER 7

DON VARDEMAN

Shared Leadership, Hard Work, Sense of Fairness
". . . Where Projects Come Together. . ."

In the three decades of IPA's existence and analysis of count-less projects and project systems, only (sadly) three project systems really stand out as having delivered sustainable and breakthrough project performance – performance that has lasted more than five years and one that has outclassed its peers by more than 25% in cost and schedule competitive-ness. That performance belongs to Anadarko Petroleum and the architect of that performance is the central character of this chapter.

Most everyone in the oil and gas industry who is remotely familiar with Anadarko's success attributes the company's performance to its extensive use of standardization; however, that misses the point entirely because standardization is the outcome of an entire style of project delivery, not something simply applied to a problem. Standardization has been, and continues to be, tried by everyone in the industry, and yet most cannot deliver results anywhere close to Anadarko's performance. The reason is that in the case of Anadarko, the way that the project organization functions *facilitates* standard-ization and Don Vardeman is the leader responsible for cre-ating that organization. Don was at the center of building an organization that truly puts people at the center through the use of shared leadership, through a deceptively simple training, mentoring, and onboarding program for project management professionals, and through continuity of more than 40 individuals who have worked with each other for over 20 years. How did Don build the only truly project-centric organization in the industry? What is it about his background, job experiences, skills, education, and characteristics that made him who he is?

Don grew up in West Texas, the son of a school superintendent and the grandson of a cotton farmer. That upbringing instilled in Don the West Texas ethics of hard work and the first most important lesson that "if someone hires you to do a job, you just do it and find a way to do it well." Don tells a story of his first summer job, which was working as a soda jerk in a dairy mart in West Texas. "It was about 2 or 3 p.m. and I was just standing by the cash register when my dad walked in. He said, 'What are you doing, Don?'" Don responded, "Well, the lunch rush is over and we have cleaned up and there is nothing else to do and no one has given me anything else to do." That was not the right answer. Don's dad responded, "That's just not right," and made him get a broom and start sweeping since a restaurant "can always use sweeping." Those qualities of hard work, bringing the best you have to the job, and always finding ways to improve and contribute have been with Don all throughout his career and have left a mark on the projects organization he built and nurtured.

After high school, Don attended Texas A&M University, the same university as Joseph Brewer, and received his degree in electrical engineering from the same program but two years ahead of Joseph. From there Don joined Amoco, close to home in West Texas, doing a variety of oilfield jobs such as drilling and completion of oil and gas wells, reservoir engineering roles related to petroleum recovery methods, as well as fracking wells to stimulate the reservoirs for improving productivity.[1] This is also where Don got the first exposure to production facilities, which he liked a lot, and wanted to continue in that discipline. But Amoco would not allow that and expected Don to transition to and learn other disciplines first. In fact, as Don says, "Amoco was the best major university in America without a football team." Amoco would provide Don and his cohorts, at minimum, half a day training each week on some subject and in fact would require that young engineers move around a lot, try different areas, and not pigeonhole themselves.

Not surprisingly, Don is a generalist just like most of the other leaders are, although they have spent enough time being good at their domain. Overstating to make the point, in our work we have not encountered a successful large project leader who is *not* a generalist. The exposure to multiple disciplines and jobs, people, places, and perspectives that Don received at Amoco is the foundation on which a generalist can build.

There is an important lesson in here for companies today. Most companies provide specialist training and in fact more and more of our organizations are teeming with specialist functions. What we end up with is a proliferation of functional specialists who tend to bog project teams down with studies and risk averseness. Owner teams get so large that they become a significant portion of total cost and add even more by micromanaging the contractors working on the projects. It is time that we go back to providing a much broader training and exposure to multiple jobs so that we

---

[1] Some of our readers may not be aware that hydraulic fracturing of oil reservoirs is not a recent invention. It has been used to stimulate production for at least 68 years. A patent was issued for the process in 1949.

produce more generalists who can become leaders.[2] It is also important to recognize the importance of training to broaden one's perspective; unfortunately, when companies experience even a slight downturn in business, training aimed at broadening horizons is often what gets cut first![3] Ironically, at Amoco, Don was able to do anything but the thing for which he was trained – electrical engineering.

One attraction for living in West Texas was proximity to most of Don and Ann's – Don's wife's – family. Don's father-in-law, Albert Holdman, was a plant operator for a major gas transportation company. Albert worked shifts and many times Don had the chance to visit the gas plant. Albert took Don on many tours of the various plants he operated. As an operator, Albert provided valuable feedback on construction and maintenance issues in the plant. Don recalls Albert telling him, "Don't be one of 'those' engineers" who never gets operations input, but expects to send something to the field and have it work perfectly. This made a permanent impact on how Don built teams and always worked to make sure the projects would work when they got to the field.

Despite the benefits, not satisfied with his inability to practice electrical engineering at Amoco, which "he nibbled on for a bit," Don accepted a headhunter's offer to move for an

---

[2] In fact, how many of today's oil and gas project leaders, who typically come from a production facilities background, could say that they worked in well construction and reservoir engineering disciplines? Their one-dimensional, specialist view makes it harder to understand other disciplines on a project and build an integrated multidisciplinary approach.

[3] There are two types of training provided by industrial firms. The more common sort is training to deepen one's knowledge of their specialty. This function-specific training is very important to maintain and develop functional competence in the staff. The other sort is training to broaden the horizons of future leaders. This sort of training is typically cut immediately when conditions soften, in part because it is often externally provided and therefore feels more expensive to the firm.

electrical engineering position at a paper mill. The paper mill was located about 600 miles east of Midland, Texas, in Orange, Texas. Orange is about as far east as you could go from West Texas, right at the border of Texas and Louisiana.

Don joined a project in the middle of construction, which allowed him to be involved in the construction, installation, and startup of a large paper machine with DC drives. The plant had one existing paper machine of about the same size and together the new plant could make a 22-foot-wide paper each day that "could spread from Orange (Texas) to El Paso (Texas)," a distance of over 800 miles (1300 km). This position was a heaven for an electrical engineer and an excellent learning opportunity for a young engineer who lived only 5 miles from the plant as opposed to the chief superintendent, who lived about 40 miles from the plant. Don's proximity to the plant meant that he was the first one at the plant during many significant outages or other unplanned events that arose at the plant and had to make critical decisions before the chief superintendent arrived to approve the plan. Don's proximity to the plant also meant that he had more frequent interactions with the hourly electrical workforce at the plant. Not only did this workforce interaction provide Don with field-level operations experience, but it also provided him with experience in leadership and, most importantly, having been involved in the construction and startup of the plant, he was also able to see how his earlier decisions played out during operations and therefore the importance of making early project decisions with the long-term end in mind.

This ability to see and relate outcomes to decisions and practices from the planning stages is a critical developmental step in a leader's ability to understand, process, and synthesize cause and effect quickly and effectively. After about two years of working for the paper mill, Don applied for an electrical engineering position at a Sun Oil Company subsidiary, Sun Exploration and Production Company (Sun E&P), to work as an electrical engineer at one of its district offices in Midland, Texas. This move started him on his path to project leadership that would one day leave a mark on the entire oil and gas industry.

Sun Oil Company had received the last offer put out by the State of California to build a cogeneration (cogen) plant and had started the complex process of getting a project through the regulatory maze to build one. So, after four years on the job in Midland, Don was dispatched on temporary assignment to Sun E&P headquarters in Dallas, TX, to relieve the chief electrical engineer while he was on vacation. During that time, he attended a presentation to company leadership about the exciting project that Sun was planning to undertake, the cogen plant to be built in Bakersfield, California, deep in the heart of the San Joaquin Valley. Seeing the complexity of the project made a mark on Don. As it happened, Don knew, as his boss had told him, that to grow his career he would have to leave Midland at some point. The cogen project was the opportunity to leave Midland and Don requested to be assigned to that project. After several months, Don got the opportunity to work on the largest capital project built by Sun Oil Company (up to that point) in the United States and he moved to California.

At the airport in Los Angeles on his way to Bakersfield, he met the person who was to be his boss – Ed Western. As Don says, "Besides my dad, grandfather, and father-in-law ... Ed changed me more than anybody." As a mentor, Ed had a large influence on Don's thinking, decision making, and approach to people and projects. As we have seen in Chapter 6 and will see in all the leadership profiles, one or two mentors play a significant role in each of our leaders' lives, and that underscores the importance of ensuring that up-and-coming leaders get exposure to a diverse set of mentors. The other theme related to mentoring that comes through in all the profiles is that all the mentors are not in the same line of growth trajectory as our leader. They are not looking for similar jobs, functions, or specialties as the mentees, which probably makes them much more effective mentors. And again, Don's mentors, like Joseph Brewer's, were mentors by mutual choice, not by corporate selection.

Don gives an anecdote of when he and Ed first met at the LAX airport. Ed asked, "Don, why do you think you are here [on this project]?" Don replied, "I don't know. I asked for it, but my boss just laughed at it and I just sort of gave up. But then I got the call and I was really happy to get a shot." Ed responded, "Don, you are known [in the company] as the young guy who has absolutely all the answers or at least thinks he does and I am known as the guy in the company who will not make a quick decision. That's why you're here. So, let's just agree that while we are here each of us will try to move toward the other's position a bit." As Don relates this anecdote, it is clear that this singular moment was what transformed the way Don thought about projects. As Don says, "Having your new boss tell you within minutes of meeting that you don't know much, this is a new world [of projects] for you, and you need to listen, understand, and help [me] make decisions and get to closure" was humbling. Of course, the lesson here, the one that Don took to heart, was that at the end of the day making decisions *is the job* of the project leader and to make good decisions the leader has to know enough about a lot of things (generalist) and surround himself with team members (specialists) who will help in decision making.

That project and the role of overall engineering manager where Don was responsible for the entire project from soup to nuts was the crucible that forged the project development and leadership model that eventually delivered a string of successes. The project team was composed of Ed Western as the overall project director, Don was the engineering manager, and a whole host of contractors, responsible for permitting, engineering, and construction, reported to Don. The full-time Sun E&P employees in the project team included about a dozen people in several disciplines. Additional full-time employees were seconded from Sun's 50% partner, Southern California Edison. Hundreds of Sun E&P and Edison employees participated as needed to support the project needs. That, more or less, reliance on a well-qualified supply chain of experienced, specialist providers working together with a minimal but extremely competent owner team is essentially the same model that Don nurtured, optimized, and tweaked and that delivered success at Kerr-McGee and later at Anadarko Petroleum. The approach to projects and people that was in place at Kerr-McGee and Anadarko under Don's leadership can be traced back to his time in California and the experiences and perspectives gained there.

For the cogen plant, the project team had to file a significant amount of paperwork related to the Environmental Impact Assessment (EIA) as well as various permits and approvals for biological resources studies, endangered species study, etc. This was all part of California Energy Commission's (CEC) major plant permitting requirements. The entire permitting paperwork amounted to a five-foot-tall stack of documents that the team had to submit and then provide testimony to support. Given the paperwork, the CEC used a contractor to review the submittals and paperwork prior to the oral testimony. However, in the midst of all this, the CEC decided to change out the contractor reviewing all of the submittals from Sun Oil Company.

With a new incoming project manager (PM) for the new contractor, the possibility of delays loomed large and Don and Ed Western decided that "we need to index and cross reference the 400 questions we have received thus far and responses to those questions and present that to the new PM." When the surprised PM at the CEC contractor asked, "You would do that for us?" Don's response was, "No, we do that for us! If we don't make your job easier, we won't get our permits [in time]." That philosophy of not simply waiting for events to unfold but to lead, take charge — and more importantly understand the end goal and the big picture — is at the core of Don's leadership style. He understood that although indexing all the responses would create extra work and cost in the short term, the project would benefit in the long run. Furthermore, being helpful builds relationships and relationships are essential to success.

Those same traits of focusing on the big picture and end goal and not waiting for events to unfold were evident two years ago when a pipeline contractor in Gulf of Mexico was late for Anadarko's project, due to a vessel being held up at another company's project. Rather than play blame games and use contractual terms and conditions to force a decision, Don's project leader knew to evaluate contingencies to avoid significant delays. The PM of the project worked with the contractor to come up with alternative solutions and found a vessel to lay the pipe so as not to delay the project. Any claims would be settled later through discussions and fairness.

Prior to coming to California, Don had largely worked in Texas and coming to California he realized that he did not know everything and certainly did not know anything about working in California. Working with a California-based utility was also a different challenge, but keeping Ed Western's words from their meeting at the airport in mind, Don backed off, swallowed his pride as the operator, got out of the way, and just let his partners and contractors, who had more experience in California, contribute. As Don states, this is where he formulated his maxim, which is: *see everything, overlook a lot, and correct a little.* As he says, "Most people will surprise you and exceed your expectations if we simply accept the fact that [things have] to be done but don't always have to be done my way."

Those 25 or so words sum up what we believe is the single most important difference between Don's project leadership style and approach to projects and that of many other major oil and gas company project leaders. In those companies, it precisely has to be their way; it has to be their work process, their technical standards, and their organizational norms. And that is why Sun Oil Company, Oryx (a spin-off from Sun), Kerr-McGee (acquirer of Oryx), and Anadarko Petroleum (acquirer of Kerr-McGee) – all the companies along Don's journey – were so successful in achieving supply chain collaboration, standardization, effective yet minimal owner teams, and – the most critical element of all – cross-functional collaboration.

Prior to the completion of the assignment in California, his first really big complex project, Sun Oil Company spun out Oryx as a new company, keeping the cogen plant with the Oryx entity. Don moved back to Midland, Texas. During this second assignment in Midland, Don was able to work with Chuck Meloy, another one of his key mentors. Chuck was the reservoir engineer in Midland. A visionary leader in his own right, Chuck became the executive responsible for most of the projects that Don was involved in. Don says that Chuck helped him to understand the value of empowerment of the project team and its contractors, as well as nurturing Don in understanding the difference between leadership and management. This relationship was present for the balance of Chuck and Don's careers and the completion of many projects. As Chuck progressed to executive vice president of Oil and Gas at Anadarko, Don remained focused on leading projects.

In Midland, Don continued to work with several colleagues who continued through from Oryx to Kerr–McGee to Anadarko, through the mergers and acquisitions. The continuity of every one of those individuals who worked with each other for over 25 years is certainly the critical ingredient of why the model built at Sun continued to flourish at Anadarko. Today, even before the crisis in the industry, professionals staying in one organization for over 20 years is almost unheard of, let alone staying in a similar role. So how did Don achieve that in the people who worked for him? For that, we go back to Sun Oil Company and its spinoff of Oryx.

After this brief second stint in Midland, Don was asked to lead his first job offshore for Oryx, looking to "connect three offshore gas wells to *something*." Subsequent to this first deepwater subsea tieback, Oryx got involved in more deepwater offshore developments and Don became the PM for the first production spar ever built – the Neptune Spar.[4] From Neptune a unique project model was developed by Don and his colleagues that evolved in what is the spar production platform supply chain today.

In this model, the concept of shared leadership is used to assure project success. It was developed and applied at Oryx by Chuck Meloy as the asset development manager (ADM) and Don Vardeman as the project manager. Chuck was the head of the venture who was responsible for issues such as the

---

[4] For readers unfamiliar with the term, a *spar* is a floating platform for developing oil fields in very deep ocean waters. The substructure for a spar is a long cylinder placed vertically in the water. It provides both buoyancy and stability. Spars have been most widely deployed in the US Gulf of Mexico. The majority have been designed and built by Technip in a longstanding relationship, under Don Vardeman's leadership.

commercial aspects, partnership issues, and subsurface. The ADM came from the subsurface discipline – and the facility construction, permitting, contracting, and execution (the project) was handled by Don. We suppose the shared leadership model was easier to adopt because Don and Chuck had already worked together at Sun E&P Company in Midland.

That same model is still in practice at Anadarko and in fact is what IPA's research indicates is a more successful model than the norm in the industry. Many companies have tried unsuccessfully (and sometimes half-heartedly) to adapt a similar ADM-based model. After understanding the evolution of that model first-hand, we believe that imposing such a model in decentralized organizations, where the culture doesn't practice shared leadership, or where continuity of personnel is not as good, will not work. The necessary ingredient is leaders who practice shared leadership, share cultural values, and are willing to build and foster continuity of personnel. Continuity of personnel was critical to building the successful spar supply chain. The continuity of personnel to help sustain the supply chain is the result of a long-term vision and 20 years of continuous efforts starting in late 1990s. The desire for continuity in relationships drove Don's repeated use of the same contractors, fabrication yards, and vendors in the development of the spar supply chain.

In 1998, Kerr-McGee (KMG) acquired Oryx and the deepwater projects unit from Oryx moved over to KMG. In the early 2000s, KMG was working on what would eventually become the Nansen Development. The following interaction describes the essence of what made Don and his project-delivery approach successful. Chuck Meloy, who was then responsible for the deepwater business unit said, "Don, we are working on Nansen and Boomvang (another deepwater Gulf of Mexico prospect) and not sure what Gunnison (the next project) might look like, but we might end up with four or five floating systems in the Gulf of Mexico. As I look around, I only see two guys who can lead a project of this size. But at the end of this project, I would like to somehow have developed a deep bench of project managers who can lead a project of this size in the future." Think about that for a moment. An ADM, with subsurface domain knowledge, working with the facility manager to create a plan that is not only focused on the project at hand but actually thinking about the next four or five opportunities and for the long-term health of the company. One cannot teach such shared leadership and vision and interaction. It cannot be mandated. It can only be fostered by the right culture, the right people, and having people trust each other – and the only way to earn trust is to work with the people over a long term. Following this interaction, Don and Chuck put in motion a brilliant recruiting program that is responsible for a supply chain of effective megaproject leaders. As Peter Drucker says, the executive first encounters the challenge of strength in staffing. The effective executive fills positions and promotes on the basis of what a person can do.[5]

The recruitment program that Don created was built for specific and strategic hiring. Each individual who was recruited into the projects organization at KMG, and then at Anadarko, was hired to fill a specific gap or skillset, such as installation or construction management expertise, that was missing in the projects organization. These skillset gaps were systematically identified by understanding the lessons from most recently completed projects and assessing the gaps and competencies that could have helped execution of those

---

[5] Peter F. Drucker, *The Effective Executive* (New York: HarperCollins, 1967).

projects. Once the individual was hired, he or she was generally a lifer and would be groomed individually and exposed to a variety of assignments on the journey to eventually becoming a project director. In fact, most of the younger project managers who worked for Don grew up the same way that Don did starting in Amoco.

Each hire started by doing a piece of a project (in their domain) and then moving on to mini-projects before being in charge of the entire project on their own – essentially an apprenticeship program that not only teaches the technical skills, but more importantly inculcates in each professional the values, culture, shared leadership model, and importance of the supply chain. This approach to hiring and training project professionals is what created the long-lasting continuity in the project leaders who worked for Don in all the organizations. As one can surmise from this, many people joined the ranks as midcareer hires. The program has also been used for recruiting new graduates with more flexibility in the early career job assignments, with a decision made later in the individuals' development on their desire for a projected-centered career.

This approach to nurturing relationships and building a loyal group of people to rely on was extended to suppliers and contractors. The same values of building trust, relationships, and continuity are what are at the heart of successful installation of so many spar projects. In fact, Oryx was part of the joint industry project (JIP) along with two other companies that funded the production spar development.

A set of suppliers and contractors came with the JIP and essentially those same contractors and suppliers are the ones who built all eight spars for Don, before he retired. That is another 20-plus-year supply chain relationship built on trust, continuity of people, shared leadership and values – rather than on legalese and iron-clad terms and conditions.[6]

In fact, the story goes that the long-standing, and still existing, alliance relationship with a subsea provider dates back continually over 20 years to the days of Oryx Energy Company and that alliance agreement was based on a single sheet of paper. Successful leaders have foresight, long-term vision, and an eye on the horizon. Don mentions "a wise VP at Oryx who told me that we will need a whole lot of subsea trees in the future so you better find someone whom you can trust and build a relationship with them so we can get the trees when we need them." He also said, "[the contract] cannot be more than a page or I will send you back." This just underscores that the mentors and senior leaders that Don learned under were visionaries, had long-term foresight, and fundamentally believed in the power of trusting people on the basis of long-term relationships.

That same view has carried through in Don and the other project managers he mentored. In fact, when asked about how he deals with team members or even contractors and vendors who are not performing, Don responds that, "Occasionally, we have some really hard conversations. I can have a much tougher conversation with someone who I have a long-standing relationship with than with another contractor who is only here for one job. That's why we have done so much relationship contracting. Because when some problem does arise, the relationship is there to talk about it. Our team is always going to treat you fairly and as long as you know that you won't get everything you want, you

---

[6] Of the owner firms in the Joint Industry Program, Oryx was the first adopter of production spar technology. Others followed after the Neptune spar was put into operation by Oryx but never caught up with the lead that first adoption generated.

will get something that we both agree is fair. There is an understanding in my organizations and all the people that work with me that we don't want to harm the contractors that are working for us. We don't want [them] to fail. When I negotiate [my] first job [with a contractor] I am looking for what will be potentially 20 years' worth of work. It may not be 20 years continuously, but we are thinking that way."[7]

Cooperating with suppliers and relationship-based contracting are buzzwords nowadays as the industry is going through a tough recalibration. Customized standards are giving way to industry and supplier-led solutions. Having learned from other great leaders, colleagues, and mentors the values-based approach to people and projects, Don was already practicing these things long before they became buzzwords and has been mentoring others in his organizations in the same approach. In fact, it is believed that one of the contributing factors for Anadarko's purchase of Kerr–McGee was for its company values system and the role values play in the business and delivery of projects.[8]

So why can't anyone else in the industry replicate this successful model? Why aren't other project leaders in the industry able to generate a supply chain that is going strong for 20-plus years? Why haven't others been able to produce a training program that produces project managers who stay around for 20-plus years, grow up in the organization, and espouse the same leadership qualities? The answer, we believe,

---

[7] Recall Joseph Brewer's statement that the more often a leader "says 'thank you' and means it" the more effective those hard discussions become. Don is making the same point.

[8] The role of values in business is discussed by Jim Hackett, the CEO of Anadarko at the time of Kerr-McGee acquisition, in the article, *Faith in Leadership*, Harvard Divinity School, November 22, 2016.

lies in the fact that they do not have leaders with character-istics and experiences like Don and, moreover, even if they do, as certainly the leaders we have profiled in this book do have those qualities, they do not work in organizations that have a strong culture of shared leadership and a values-based approach to projects and people.

About five years ago, we invited Don to speak to 200 or so of our clients at our annual exploration and production (E&P) company conference. We asked Don to talk about what in his mind made him successful and, also, what is at the core of truly and probably the only fully project-centric model in the industry. Don described in detail their values-based approach to projects. He described how they select profes-sionals, their apprenticeship-type training, and how the val-ues of relationships and fairness are drilled into the project people, including clarity through action examples in which younger project managers observe senior leaders maintaining fairness in negotiations with contractors to build long-lasting relationships.

Well, almost every major oil company attendee and some senior leaders from the largest oil companies in the room scoffed at this soft stuff. Such soft things don't help; they sound nice but there is nothing substantive, they claimed. Of course, fast forward to today and here are those same companies struggling to finish their projects on time and on budget, having to now conduct significant layoffs, and struggling to reinvent themselves as low-cost organizations, while Don's project organization flourished with the soft stuff. What, in fact, didn't work was the process-driven, rather than people-driven, approach to projects and the lack of leadership and culture in the other organizations.

The characteristics that made Don the most effective project leader were very simple. He developed relationships of trust with the people around him and then let them do the work their own way as long as it was done well. He got out of the way. He coached a lot – coached on the value of relationships, of fairness, and of shared leadership. He selected people to work for him based on their values. More importantly, he, along with two other Sun colleagues who were at higher positions than him in the most recent job, created and fully protected a culture in which people felt comfortable bringing problems to their superiors. This is an example of understanding the notion of psychological safety in action. It creates stronger teams.

Creating the environment in which problems are allowed to surface without fear of embarrassment is known as psychological safety in the literature.[9] Psychological safety is essential for teams to function effectively. One aspect of generating psychological safety is ensuring that everyone on a team has the opportunity to be heard. As we discussed in Chapters 4 and 5, one of the essential characteristics of successful complex project leaders is their willingness to listen to everyone's view. Don Vardeman, who benefited from mentors such as Ed Western and others, intuitively understood the concept of psychological safety and was able to build strong and highly capable teams as a result. Until he retired, Don mentored and coached all sorts of people, even professionals in disciplines far from his own.

It is said that a leader is someone who brings out the best in the people who work for him. A leader is someone who knows the direction and the destination but doesn't have page-by-page directions and is willing to accept various ways of reaching the goal. A leader is someone who always has

---

[9] Amy Edmondson, "Psychological Safety and Learning Behavior in Work Teams," *Administrative Science Quarterly* 44, no. 2 (June 1999): 350–383.

his eyes on the horizon and is working for the long term. A leader is humble, one who recognizes that he does not have all the answers and is willing to surround himself/herself with knowledgeable people and listen to them. A leader provides the moral compass within which the organizational culture takes shape. Those are all the characteristics that Don has and more importantly that all the other leaders he has trained have.

CHAPTER 8

NORA'IN MD SALLEH AND DZULKARNAIN AZAMAN

Conquering Functional Dysfunction

We are now going to pivot from a project-centered organization in Texas to a function-centered system in Southeast Asia. The cultures of the nations are quite different. The cultures of the companies are quite different. But the basics of complex project leadership are going to look much the same.

Nora'in Salleh and Dzulkarnain Azaman are successful complex project leaders at the same company, a prominent Asian national oil company. We have combined our conversations with Nora'in and Dzul because the challenges facing them as project leaders in a national company are the same and their approaches, although different, are complementary.

The project systems of virtually all national oil companies are organized into functional departments. This form of organization probably derives from their government ownership because government departments are similarly organized. Each function, which represents a small portion of the total project process, tends to jealously guard its part of the pie, controlling both monetary and people resources. Generating adequate cross-functional cooperation is very difficult even in organizations that are strong-matrixed. In a functionally organized world, generating cross-functional cooperation approaches the heroic. Both of these project leaders found ways to overcome those challenges.

NORA'IN MD SALLEH

"When people ask me what good leadership is, three things come to my mind straight away. The first, in order for you to be considered a good leader you must be able to make a decision and stand by it. Second, as a leader, if you are not calm and stable enough but rather skittish and jumpy, you will discourage people from coming to you and explaining and sharing their issues with you.[1] The third one is walk the talk. Because in projects it's really very important for you to be in the shoes of your team and your contractors and only then will you be able to form good cooperation among the team." This response is typical of good project leaders. What is not typical is that this leader is a woman, in a male-dominated society at a national oil company in Asia. Nora'in Salleh is a standout performer.

National oil companies are almost always functionally siloed; that is to say, the functions become a unit and the inter-actions across various units are across the functional or unit boundaries. Each function has its tools, processes, and people residing in the function and the people are often matrixed in or loaned to the project team rather than forming an integrated and dedicated project group. The team members' hard-line reporting is to their functional leader rather than the project leader. It is very rare for the project leader to even be asked for input into the team members' performance eval-uation. In such functionally based project systems, the leader must cultivate followership in all team members. The leader cannot function by trying to be the boss because the project leader in such systems is not the boss. The functional managers are the bosses. Rather, cooperation must be earned through

---

[1] This is an illustration of the emotional intelligence skill of being able to put others at ease that we found highly correlated with project success.

leadership. We asked Nora'in how she thought a leader should pick her team members. She replied, "That's a tough one, because people are assigned to me. I never get to pick them." In functionally based systems, the mettle of leadership is fully tested. There is no formal power on which to fall back.

One of the key attributes in getting people to be on your side is to build trust through integrity and reliability. Nora'in's approach to building trust illustrates those attributes. She starts building open communication channels within her team by being present. Shortly after a project kickoff, Nora'in visits with each and every discipline (remember, this is a functionally based organization) to give an update on the project, the cost, schedule, and other relevant issues, as well as the goals, vision, and mission of the project. Her updates cover all relevant aspects of the mission even if they are not directly related to the discipline she is visiting. Note that she visits them; she doesn't call them to her office.

In essence, what Nora'in is doing here is building a sense of community in the various functions and encouraging them to see themselves as part of something larger than their function. By visiting the disciplines rather than asking the disciplinary representatives to visit her, she is displaying the humility that is common in the most effective leaders. By volunteering information in a culture in which information is power, she is earning their trust. She then can become the glue that will hold the community together; even though the functions may not cooperate or talk to each other, they will through her because she has earned their trust through "walking the talk." Over time, having seen the benefits of information sharing, the functions start sharing information with Nora'in and other functions on their own. Nora'in has demonstrated the behaviors she expects others to emulate.

Another small behavior that helps build trust is an element of empathy. What is different is how Nora'in interacts with people on her team. Unlike other managers, she goes out of her office and approaches them in their cubicles rather than asking them to come to her office to give them updates. As Nora'in says, "I find that if I go to their space they are more relaxed and open so the communication flows more naturally and they are feeling that I am more close to them and are willing to open up and tell me the story about their progress. Even at fabrication sites I make it a point that I am there at least two days a week ... and I follow the same approach where I don't sit there in an office but go approach them at their work stations."

This may appear unremarkable to most readers, but it is absolutely critical to understand the context in which Nora'in is displaying these traits. Although this open-door approach may be more common in Western companies,[2] hierarchies matter a lot in a national oil company and the typical situation is that you go to your superior's office to report. This behavior by Nora'in in a national oil company (NOC) environment turns that paradigm on its head and probably helps her get people on her side.

So how did Nora'in develop these skills? As Joseph Brewer reminded us, "The hard (technical) stuff is easy; it's the soft stuff that's hard!" It may be that women are taught how to do the soft stuff earlier and better than men, but Nora'in's professional background seems quite similar to many of the successful male leaders we have met.

Nora'in started her career not at an NOC but in a company that did not have many large projects at the time. The company was concentrating on brownfield projects using an engineering-managed modifications model, whereby one

---

[2] As an aside, although the open-door policy may be discussed and talked about a lot in Western world, we doubt how much of that is actually practiced in the true sense of the word.

project engineer handled several brownfield modifications. That meant the project engineer needed to know the overall scope and also needed to secure support from other disciplines to ensure successful outcomes. Nora'in's first exposure to the world of project management was in charge of costs, schedules, procedures, and safety. It was also her first exposure to building the skills necessary to get people on her side in the workplace. Throughout the execution of these projects, if she needed help from a particular discipline she would have to reach out to the various functions to get help from the subject-matter experts and advisers, who resided in functions. This experience is actually not unlike that of the other leaders we meet in other chapters – package manager, brownfield manager – who served in the role of project manager for smaller projects and built their domain knowledge (by necessity) in disciplines other than theirs, and also built and enhanced their skills in getting people to work with them collaboratively. This is how Nora'in strengthened her domain knowledge and became an expert in her discipline first.

Nora'in perfected her discipline of project management by leading the engineering-managed modifications, but we believe the attributes that make her a fox were developed in her second job, working for a regulatory agency in which she was essentially working as a non-operating liaison and observing a variety of other operators develop and execute their projects. The value of a non-operating role as a critical learning experience in project leadership was discussed in Chapter 4. The aspiring leader is always a learner; the watching role is an unparalleled learning opportunity for those willing to make good use of it.

As an overseer of operators' compliance to the regional guidelines, Nora'in had the unique vantage point of observing the good and bad approaches to project management by a variety of project teams from a number of companies both national and international. This foundational experience early in her career exposed her to a wide range of difficult situations commonly encountered in projects. She was able to assess which ways of approaching problems and finding solutions resulted in positive outcomes and which approaches, styles, and methods disrupt the project. In fact, being an open leader, Nora'in was not just satisfied being an observer and she would help the project teams that were under her purview, go on site visits with them, and participate actively in team meetings. This undoubtedly allowed her to observe positive and negative traits, including how different companies, different cultures, and even different project teams from the same company and culture deal with people, contractors, and stakeholders (her role). These learnings, as Nora'in says, are what really helped her develop her people management skills. This also helped her to develop her own set of best practices that she carries to the next project and to adapt her style along the way. As Henry Ford said, the only real mistake is the one from which we learn nothing.

Nora'in's learning model is similar to the other successful leaders: collect and curate a catalog of her personal best practices as she moved from one project to the next. When she encounters difficult issues or problems on a project, her approach is not always to find the root cause of the problem, but to do just enough investigation to quickly find a solution, fix it, and move on. After the problem is solved, she sits with the relevant parties to understand any specific root causes and to distill best practices that get recorded in her personal collections after any necessary sharing with the relevant stakeholders has happened. In this way Nora'in is able to round out and refine the lesson she has learned. But, as Nora'in says, for a lesson to enter her personal best practice collection on what to do (or not to do), she needs "some time for me to sink it in... Not too long, maybe about a day ... but that 'sink-in' time is extremely important to me and if I don't get it, I won't be able to solve the problem for myself to carry a learning forward." As we discussed back in Chapter 4, good leaders tend to be a reflective lot.

We have seen that all the leaders discussed thus far have had similar experiences, opportunities, and career trajectories that gave them the opportunity to build their knowledge and skills. We have also discussed that the leader often started out as a disciplinary specialist but was driven by his or her foxy nature to want more. Then what role, if any, does the organization play in the making and success of a project leader? How much of a leader's success is about personality and how much is it about the role of the organization? Said differently, what sort of environment is necessary for a project leader to succeed or for a young professional to evolve into a project leader?

An organization that is "open and willing" is how Nora'in described the right environment for a leader to flourish. Of course, just as with people, openness in an organization is a measure of whether the organization is a learning organization − willing to change with the times, willing to adapt to a changing context, willing to be flexible in the face of unique and new circumstances, and willing to learn from its past lessons and renew and transform[3] itself. Nora'in proved that good leadership can generate learning even in the difficult environment of a functionally based system by taking everyone's desire to achieve a great outcome and fashion

---

[3] We avoided the word *reorganization* here because it has become a euphemism for letting people go and doesn't really have anything to do with reorganizing for the better. We have always wondered how reorganizing by shedding key resources is a winning strategy.

that into the spirit of cooperation needed to succeed against the odds.

DZULKARNAIN AZAMAN

Dzul started his career as an electrical engineer working for a utility company that sponsored his education in the UK.[4] After working for the company for about two years, he accepted a job as a wireline engineer with an oil field services company. In a typical service provider career fashion, Dzul spent the next few years working as a wireline engineer in Indonesia, Egypt, and then in the United States. We believe that this exposure to different people, different cultures, and different work environments is essential in broadening a person's perspective and making him more open, willing, and receptive to other people's views, opinions, and contributions. Surely this experience and exposure played a role in Dzul's approach to building a team that brought together diversity in many forms to tackle a project with technological challenges and a stretch target.

After a few years as a wireline engineer Dzul decided to join a NOC, and he was put in a functional organization given his engineering background. He was then assigned to a project as an electrical engineer. On the project, Dzul moved from the design engineering office to the fabrication yard, participated in the hookup and commissioning (HUC), and then moved on to the operations phase. As we were talking about his early years and how he became an expert in his domain and got exposure to project management, Dzul said something that is critically important and has a bearing on how we move project

---

[4] As neither author is an electrical engineer, we want to assure the readers that this apparent pattern of electrical engineers (3 of 7 profiled here) being successful complex leaders is nothing more than a statistical fluke.

team members today. He said, "As I was not born and raised in this organization, toward the end of the project, right after the completion of the HUC activities, everyone started looking to move on to other projects. For me, I was not in that mode and so I stayed on the project as I was familiar with [it]. Since most of the senior project management folks had started to leave for other work, I was assigned to handle the punch-list items. As a young engineer, with no senior staff around, I had to now familiarize myself and work with contracts and commercial terms more closely [to ensure completion of punch list]. That was my first exposure to project management. I was also provided a group of young engineers to develop and to ensure completion of punch-list items. I had to work with them and manage the interaction and work with the operations group. That was my first exposure to total project management."

This early experience, totaling about six years, is similar to what we have seen in the early careers of the other leaders. A solid grounding in fundamentals of their domain with exposure to the world of project management is followed by management of smaller scale mini-projects and more importantly seeing projects from end to end, which provides the learning of seeing one's design, engineering, and project management decisions play out in the field. In today's world, or at least the world of projects until about mid-2014, an average professional would be in a job for maybe three years before moving to a different position on a new project or in a new organization. Most of the project team members would start to leave even before the project was fully complete, including the project manager, who in many cases was already transitioning to another project. This model may suffice for those who have already established themselves as accomplished project professionals, but this model certainly does not provide enough opportunity for young future leaders to achieve a strong foundation in a particular domain. If one never gets the chance to actually see how decisions turn out, it is hard to build learnings that one can carry to the next venture. All our leaders had solid grounding in end-to-end project management and that is something that needs to be brought back, which of course will require us to rethink today's project organizations and career models.

After his stint on the project, Dzul was then assigned to another project – as senior electrical engineer – in a frontier region of the world where he progressed through senior electrical engineer, then a resident engineer, and finally company site representative at the project design office, overseeing all aspects of the design and coordinating with other company site representatives, the project manager, and the project team in-country.

Dzul's next step was a big one. He was selected to be the executive assistant and planner for the CEO of the company where he was exposed to human resource discussions and financial issues as well. In this role Dzul was able to see a variety of project managers present the merits of their projects to the CEO. He could watch and learn firsthand positive and negative project leadership traits, including differentiating project leaders who have breadth and depth, and seeing firsthand how a project leader with breadth can handle risk-related discussions with the CEO far more deftly than a project leader who is competent but lacking in breadth.

This unique role also enabled Dzul to build a network of relationships across the organization. Most of the successful project leaders we interviewed had found some way to build a network of people across their organization as part of their early careers. Such networks become a lifeline when difficulties arise with a project and a favor is needed. Networks are particularly important in organizations such as Dzul's that are functionally siloed because cooperation is not normative in such companies. In a real sense, generating a successful complex project requires finding ways around the company's formal norms and requirements so that cooperation rather than functional rivalry can prevail.

Although not explicitly stated by Dzul, surely his network and the relationships made during his tenure as an assistant to CEO had an influential and smoothing role in convincing the organization to try out unorthodox approaches to managing projects. Dzul does agree, however, that getting a breadth of experience is what makes him a more holistic project leader than other project managers who take a hands-off approach when dealing with reservoir or construction domains. Dzul sees the role of a leader as connector of functions and thoughts or in his words "an integrator or perhaps a communicator."

Dzul was handed the project leader position for a complex, fast-tracked, economically marginal project, which is probably every project leader's least favorite type of project. At the time this project was being planned and conceptualized, the oil market was still at its peak (no one foresaw that within months the market would collapse). Generally speaking, the project leader does not get to select his own team in Dzul's company, unlike the usual international company. However, given the nature of the project and its resource constraints, Dzul recommended that the organization use a project management contractor (PMC) model. This was Dzul's approach to circumventing the constraints imposed by the system.

A PMC concept is not new to the industry and was also not entirely new in this organization; it was, however, the first time it would be applied to an oil production project. The organization, culturally, was not ready for this concept because

NORA'IN MD SALLEH AND DZULKARNAIN AZAMAN 161

it requires people from outside of the organization who may not be familiar with the way the organization works. Dzul had to convince senior management in the organization that the PMC concept would work. He did that by communicating the way he would manage the PMC to alleviate the organization's fears and the organization was willing to try a new concept given the project's time constraints. The organization was willing to be flexible and adapt its way once presented with a cogent argument and data. This is fairly atypical, especially for a national oil company.

Given the risks and fears expressed by the organization, Dzul requested CVs of all the personnel who were proposed. He read them and personally interviewed each one of the potential team members, not once but twice. These interviews weren't delegated to human resources or someone else on the team. The goal of the interviews was to build a team – by design – that would be suitable for that project's unique context, as well as for the organization it was in. This is an illustration of how a leader needs to understand the unique context of the venture and also understand the blend of skills required for success.

Because Dzul's project was marginal, it needed to employ technology that was new to the company and not aligned precisely with the organization's technical standards. So, the interview focused on how comfortable the team members would be in thinking outside the box and working with technologies that would require a stretch of some internal standards and requirements. Would the team members be comfortable with it? Would that stretch make them less confident in their decision making? Would the PMC personnel be willing to learn the way of the organization?

But the bigger focus of Dzul's interviews was on personality, behaviors, and people skills. Not only was the PMC concept new, the engineering procurement construction and commissioning (EPCC) contractor was an American company in the middle of trying to build a relationship with Dzul's organization. This meant that the PMC contractor, who would be the acting owner, needed to be technically competent but also needed to be able to work with a Western EPCC contractor that preferred its own set of rules and technical standards. The PMC contractor needed to be experienced in construction, be able to hold its own with the EPCC contractor, communicate well in English, have established networks in the industry that it could tap into in case of problems and issues, have proven work discipline ethics, and be able to work comfortably in a stretch schedule environment. Dzul also focused on staffing the team, not just with locals, but with team members from several different countries who would bring together a diversity of thought and ideas.

As is well documented in literature, a team that is composed of diverse skills, behaviors, personalities, and experiences is probably more open to try new ideas, approaches, and methods and is more accepting of divergent views, which can often produce radical and breakthrough ideas. The fact that Dzul focused on that aspect in building a team shows that he, just like the other leaders we have met, understands the first principle of projects, which is that people do projects. In this debate about how much role an organization plays in the success of a leader, this issue of divergent thinking is a critical one.

Leaders don't become leaders unless they have followers. The only way to build followers is communication. The greater the size and complexity of a project and the greater the number of functions in an organization, the greater the difficulty of ensuring communication but the more it is necessary for the effective functioning of projects. Nora'in and Dzul have an important lesson for us. Effective leaders can often manage to overcome intrinsically difficult circumstances to produce excellent results. These two leaders found ways to create functioning project teams in an environment that does not foster teamwork. Each had their unique approach but the result was the same: excellent teams producing excellent projects.

CHAPTER 9

JAY SEXTON

Clarity of Vision, Clarity Through Action, Staffing for Success
"In general, I like to keep driving."

The following scenario is all too common in the oil and gas industry: an offshore platform is being fabricated in a yard, and the owner has people in the yard acting as eyes and ears, as thousands of workers scramble around the emerging ship, when out of the blue the fabricator announces that the vessel will be six months late to completion. Anyone familiar with offshore industry now knows that this project is in a world of trouble. Either the vessel will leave the yard with six months of work yet to be done, which will cost at least five times more to complete at sea than in the yard, or the sail–away date is slipped with a severe penalty to the project's cost. Depending on availabilities in other parts of the supply chain, the project will now be 6 to as much as 12 months late. Jay Sexton simply was not willing to accept such an outcome without exhausting every possibility first.

Our project leader, upon discovery of this schedule slippage, got directly involved and started going to the fabrication yard every week. For the first few weeks, he held daily and weekly meetings with every one of the disciplines working in the yard on his project. His purpose, as he explained it, "was to self-understand how the disciplines planned to do the work. Since I don't know how they do the work and since I don't know how this yard's process and procedures work, I can't help them. I want to build trust with the disciplines and once they explain how their work is done I can understand, then maybe I can start helping." One of the examples he gave us was in one of the discipline areas; after talking to the yard personnel, he realized that they needed at least two more people to finish the work and he – the owner project leader – directed the yard to hire more people. The yard was working under a fixed price contract. Think about that for a minute and then let's step back and explain what would normally happen in this scenario.

Typically, such an intervention by an owner into the contractor's work would be considered as interference and all impact that could possibly be attributed to the said intervention would be grounds for significant claims that the contractor would seek from the owner. Any lawyer, purchasing, or contracts person would advise against such intervention and because of that, or because most project managers would accept their fate, the project is going to fail.

Going back to our fabrication yard, our leader told the contractor project manager to "go get the people and send me the bill. But, I want to pick up the pace." In hearing our leader tell this story, it was clear that the contractor project manager (PM) was skeptical and so our leader had to assure him that the path laid out was the right one and to at least try it. If it didn't work out, the leader would pay the bill, but if it did and the schedule is recovered, he was "not sure what bill the contractor will submit to the owner given that there will be 'savings.'" In some cases, it was the owner's people at the site team who were indecisive and holding up things and our leader fixed those issues as well, which helped convince the yard management and yard personnel that the project leader was balanced and fair and had only one goal – to recover the schedule and complete the project in the best possible manner. After the yard intervention, the project leader and the managing director of the yard had standing weekly phone calls until the end.

The project recovered all of the six-month delay, sailed offshore, and recovered time offshore as well. In fact, the yard management and personnel say, "This was the best project we ever worked on." Although the owner has a view, it illustrates how a leader who shows clarity of vision through action, was fair, and focused on people and not processes can rally everyone and end up delivering a positive feeling and positive outcome. Contrast this with how the situation arose in the first place.

The site team working for the owner was receiving weekly project status data and one has to believe that they knew that the project was falling behind. However, either due to inappropriate optimism or misinterpretation of the data, they believed the project could be recovered until it was too late. Upon discovery, when the project leader asked them what the solution was, their response was, "We are going to write them [the contractor] a letter every day to tell them they are late." As our leader responded, "They know and we know they are late! What are we going to do about it?" "It's not our fault, it's theirs, and so they have to fix it," was the response. This exchange, by the way, is how many project managers respond; they cling to the process, they cling to the structure, and they cling to the systems. Jay, on the other hand, likes to drive, take actions, and find solutions, which is precisely what he did. In fact, because the project was late, toward the end it was also apparent that the project would need to hire some expeditors to ensure that the recovered schedule wasn't lost in the middle of offshore hookup and commissioning. Sensing the reluctance of the contractor, Jay hired an expatriate hedgehog expeditor, who worked for the contractor and reported to the contractor project manager but whose salary for the entire duration was paid for by Jay. That shows a tremendous amount of integrity and dedication to the mission at hand.

While Jay was fixing the delay, every week letters would go back and forth on each side – keeping the lawyers employed and happy – until the project was done. At the end, when it was time to settle the claims, Jay and his counterpart, along with their teams, collected all the letters and sat together to go through each of the hundreds of letters and make a call one by one. As Jay said, that approach must have been a good method of fair and balanced claim settlement because at the end, "both sets of teams were unhappy because they got a bad deal." More amazing is that no corporate lawyers from the owner side were involved in this settlement, which would be anathema in most organizations. That speaks to the trust in Jay's leadership. Of course negotiating claims is probably a bit easier for Jay when the contractors can plainly see that he is not playing a zero-sum game and is willing to be beyond fair to them (as in the case of the expeditor).

Hopefully, this example makes clear the difference between project managers and that rarer breed – project leaders. Project managers try to optimize the status quo by focusing on the short term and the processes and systems as they currently exist. Their goal is to survive. Leaders, like Jay, on the other hand are courageous enough to take bold actions, willing to challenge norms and culture, but more importantly with their eye on the horizon and the vision they work with people – not processes – to change mindsets and behaviors.

The essential lesson from the example above, however, is the order in which things were done. First, Jay studied, learned, and understood. He knew there was no point in trying to be helpful if you don't know what you're doing! Second, he built relationships of trust with all involved: his own people working in the yard and yard management. Only then did he start to recommend and implement solutions. What leaders know is that the trust they earn is repaid in reducing the risks of the actions they take. Jay's risk was that if his solutions hadn't worked, his management would have lowered the boom on him if the yard had been able to use his intervention to wiggle out of their responsibilities. The trust developed mitigated the risk of that happening.

What Jay displays are the attributes of integrity, openness, awareness of mission, and more importantly calm and stability in face of duress. So how did Jay get here? Like most of our other successful leaders, Jay did not envision a career in project management. He started out as a petroleum engineer working in discipline areas and then slowly evolved into project management. He started out designing tank batteries, well completions, and a variety of other discipline-area scopes. Although they weren't projects and weren't part of project management, the scopes required interaction with other disciplines, which was important as it taught the skill of how to relate to other functions and provided Jay with a broader background. Essentially these were mini-projects that exposed Jay to project management prior to his move to an offshore environment overseas working with a European company in a joint-operating capacity managing packages.[1] Through demonstrated success in managing these packages, he progressed into managing 8 to 10 packages as opposed to single scope and eventually running entire large offshore teams. With slow steps of success, he progressed to larger and larger scopes,

---

[1] Packages are essentially mini-projects; subsystems that are part of larger modules. For instance, a turbine generator package, which itself will require some engineering and contain some equipment, some bulk materials, and will be part of a larger power generation module.

moving from project lead engineer positions to a project manager role.

The exposure that Jay had, working in various countries and with a variety of joint venture partners, as well as the steady progression from smaller to larger projects, has made him very comfortable with lots of moving parts. In fact, unlike most other project teams and project organizations that we encounter, Jay's teams usually do not have a dedicated interface manager position. Jay considers himself to be the interface manager, and given his calm, collected, and stable demeanor, he is not the least bit fazed with managing the interfaces or making constant decisions. In fact, Jay says, "If it's a $5 decision or $50 M decision I am not stressed about it. If the decision is the best decision that can be made in light of the data in hand, then I make the decisions and move on. I am not too stressed about missed calls either."[2]

This is the antithesis of analysis paralysis, which is what we often see in organizations that are depending on project managers and are devoid of leadership. Leaders make decisions. They do not vacillate and waiver. They recognize that their job is to make decisions for themselves and for others. Of course there are missed calls, and, in fact, in the incident described earlier, probably there were a few missed calls, including selecting a yard that was not competent and hiring people on the team — the site representatives — who were new to him and he did not have a relationship with. So how does Jay learn from his mistakes or missed calls? This learning model reveals something about the most important attribute of leaders — how

---

[2] This very much recalls our discussion in Chapter 4 about how good leaders make decisions: by gathering up all the information available and then making the decision. They don't wait; they don't agonize; they don't seek consensus; they make decisions.

they deal with people. We will discuss that after we describe the learning model.

Jay's learning model comprises three basic elements: review, understand, and take accountability. In the first step, each failure, each learning, and each missed call is thoroughly reviewed with the specialists – the engineers and technicians – who were involved in that scope. The goal of the review is to work with the subject-matter experts, to understand (second element) what was missed in the analysis that led to a missed call or failure. Were the risks just not understood well or were they, in fact, understood well but something that couldn't have been foreseen still transpired? The third element involves accountability; Jay makes the decision on the path forward and is therefore accountable for the decisions. To facilitate that, he seeks to have all the facts explained to him and if he feels like he understands the problem, then he makes the decision comfortably. For Jay, using this model ensures that the next time he finds himself in a similar situation he is not second guessing himself, or tentative in decision making.

Of course, this approach to decision making is predicated on the specialists having analyzed the problem correctly, providing the right inputs, and following the proper methodology. Then if the decision doesn't come out well, the result is chalked up to Murphy of Murphy's Law – the Patron Saint of All Projects. We suspect most good leaders are like Jay in not losing too much sleep over decisions that turned out wrong for reasons that couldn't be foreseen. For this learning model to succeed, leaders like Jay have to have a significant amount of trust and confidence in the capabilities of the people who work for them. People, not processes, do projects. And so, people matter and the leader-constituent interaction is therefore critical.[3]

---

[3] John W. Gardner, *On Leadership* (New York: The Free Press, 1990), 23–37.

Jay's approach to assembling a team for a new project is unorthodox, especially for a major oil company. Jay's company gives him the leeway to staff his teams mostly in the manner he sees fit with a combination of company people and individual contractors. Most international companies allow their project directors to select most of their own staff, but mostly from in-house employees only. Whether selecting from in-house staff or individual contractors, Jay's approach is the same. "My favorite method is to rely on references for people I hire from people I know and trust." He goes on to say, "I might hire a pipeline manager for the team without even meeting him (or her) if someone I know, trust, and respect very well has recommended the engineer to me."

In fact, he believes that when he has picked people by relying more on the CV or resume it often hasn't worked out as well as expected based on the CV. He values subject-matter experts, regardless of where they come from. Whether the person is local or expat, or any other differentiation does not matter if they are the best in their discipline. Furthermore, Jay's typical model for staffing is to rely much more on contract staff than owner personnel to build out a team because, as he puts it, "this is their livelihood and they are not locked in one way of doing things." This is an unusual approach. To make it work, Jay has to be convinced that he can generate the kind of dedication to the project that is more typical among company employees than individual contractor staff. It also seems like a commentary on the typical organization's approach to maintaining staff.

In Jay's thinking, having staff who have seen lots of problems in lots of places helps ensure success. Team members who have worked for several different operators and contractors, in several different regions of the world, and on several different kinds of projects bring together a much more divergent thinking that can be very useful in problem solving.

If the project leader is open to new ideas and others' views, then such a divergent group can come up with some very innovative, ingenious, and creative ways of solving typical project troubles. On the other hand, company lifers may be encumbered by their own internal processes and "this is how we do it here" attitudes that can be a hindrance. In this age of hyper-specialization, it is easy for staff to become too risk averse and process bound. Every innovative solution to a problem represents a form of risk-taking. If company staff become too risk averse, it is easy to see why a project leader would look for staff outside the company.

On a typical project that Jay leads, about 30 to 50% of people have worked with him on the project immediately prior and many of them are contract employees. In Jay's understanding, specialists work best when they are consulted, challenged, held in high regard, but are not charged with making the decisions. This approach has enabled Jay to gather specialists who will move mountains for him. Some so prefer working for Jay that they have quit their existing jobs to join Jay's team when he needed them.

Jay prefers to run lean teams with only six to eight direct reports. Those direct reports then hire additional people to build out their team. The direct reports pick up on the behaviors that Jay exhibits and then in turn apply similar behaviors and methods for their reports. The discipline or scope area leaders are then accountable for their own teams. The staffing-for-success model builds teams around, or dedicated to, a contract object (area of contracted scope). The teams for that contract object are responsible and accountable for everything technical, commercial, contract, cost, and schedule inside that contract object.

This is very similar to the mini-projects that Jay saw in his early days and similar to other mini-projects in the backgrounds of other leaders. The cracks between the scope areas or contract objects where things tend to fall through are the scope and scheduling interfaces that are managed by Jay. According to Jay, he spends "a significant amount of time locking those scope and schedule interfaces" and ensuring that the entire team, including all the team members from the winning contractors, are fully aware of his vision of how the project will be successfully executed. To further ensure clarity through action, each scope area or contract object team will have its own site-based cost and schedule controls group that feed in data to a central project controls group that then standardizes all tracking, measuring, and reporting metrics and dashboards, which is then fed back to the teams so everyone is working off of the same basis every time. This, by the way, was a similar model that was deployed successfully by Joseph Brewer's highly complex joint venture projects in the Middle East.

The foundation of Jay's string of successful projects then is based on his method of picking the right people – specialists (hedgehogs) with the right behaviors and characteristics, including directness and intense job focus. Jay spends a lot of time building teams by really looking at the details of each member on the team. Are they specialists or generalists? Are they broadminded or narrow-minded? How do they behave? How should the project be divided given the players I have? Having the right team is central to achieving the end goal of the project and that fits well with Jay's definition of exemplary leadership, which is "keeping the path and vision of where we want to get to, to succeed and not letting people get dispirited and bogged down in details that don't help the big picture. We are part of something bigger and cheerleading a bit and helping everyone keep an eye on the horizon."

When people quit their existing jobs to come work for Jay when needed, it shows a level of trust in Jay that is rare in the industry. Followers make a leader and for that followers need trust in their leaders. As Bennis points out, there are four ingredients leaders have that generate trust:[4]

- *Constancy:* Whatever surprises leaders themselves may face, they shield the team from them and don't create any surprises. Jay is the quintessential calm in the storm keeping the turbulence away from the team. Communication is therefore an important task for Jay in conjunction with "leave your desk," as Jay describes it. Even though you may be a leader, leaving your desk to talk to team members establishes power and following through trust, rather than through title, which makes persuasion and motivation easier when needed. Note the similarity in style to Nora'in Salleh, who takes care to visit everyone on their own turf.[5]
- *Congruity:* Leaders walk the talk. Many project managers we have encountered in our work espouse the right theories and best practices and say the right words. But in practice they do not deliver. By practicing clarity through action, Jay is actively involved in driving and managing every bit of his projects.

---

[4] Warren Bennis, *On Becoming a Leader* (New York: Basic Books, 2009), 152–153.

[5] After watching many hundreds of megaprojects succeed or fail, we are convinced that Sexton's approach of keeping distractions and headaches from outside the team away from the team is the correct approach. When teams believe the project is caught up in politics either from internal or external stakeholders, they can easily become distracted and discouraged. If the politics continually interfere with their ability to focus on their work, the team blames the project director and their confidence in the project leader is undermined. Obviously, this is a judgment call for the project leader about when to clue the team into a problem and when not to. But too many distractions clearly jeopardize the leader's standing.

- *Reliability:* Leaders are there when it counts and are ready to support their coworkers when it matters.
- *Integrity:* Leaders honor their commitments and promises. There is no better example of the last two elements than the moment when Jay hired an expeditor and paid his salary, but had him work for the contractor – essentially free help – so that the ultimate mission was successful. This also highlights another element that differentiates leaders and managers; leaders go against the corporate grain and do the right thing without always waiting to ask for permission and approval.

The fact that there aren't many, if any, other leaders in Jay's organization or the other organizations we have encountered with a similar track record of successes or similar eager constituents proves that most organizations aren't even looking to their project management professionals to spot, let alone nurture, leadership potential.

It is said that leaders invent themselves in a crucible of context.[6] Just as the Great Depression was a crucible for Franklin D. Roosevelt and World War II was for Churchill, projects are the crucible that allowed Jay to flourish as a leader. As he says, "the money we are involved with [for projects], the stress, and the criticality of these huge decisions is a responsibility that I find pretty thrilling."

---

[6] Bennis, *On Becoming a Leader*, 36.

CHAPTER 10
PAUL HARRIS

Know Thyself, Be a Collector of People, Have Your Own
Learning Model
"I am a Magpie."

If we were to take the analysis and learnings in this work and craft a deliberate plan for a young engineer to become a successful project leader, what would that plan look like? We suspect it would look a lot like the career of Paul Harris. Paul's journey from a young engineer to a top project executive provides a textbook for how one might develop a strong project leader. Paul's journey is very unusual in having such clarity and definition and foresight; it is almost as if Paul had a curated career specifically designed for him.

We first met Paul ten years ago when we were visiting him and his team for a readiness assessment of his project. The project we were reviewing was being done on the heels of another project that was recently completed by a different team, but the same organization, that had gone terribly awry. It wasn't a particularly large project – monetarily – but it was complex. As we discussed Paul's project, it was very clear from the beginning that Paul wasn't an ordinary project manager. He knew *every* detail about the project, where it stood, what the open areas of risks were, and how the team was positioned to deal with any risks that may materialize. At that point, given the recently completed project that had gone awry, we weren't entirely sure whether Paul's views were unrealistic optimism, boasting, or confidence driven by a successful track record. In any case, Paul was open, inviting, and engaging, and we hit it off and that began a professional connection that continues to this day. Today, Paul is at the top of his leadership journey and is the divisional president for his organization.

How did Paul get here? Did he have a well-defined plan for himself? A plan that charted out a path from his early days as a technical engineer to a project leader with a track record of delivering successful projects? We posed that question to Paul. His response: "No! Absolutely not! In fact, I looked at others in those roles and thought that those roles are outside the realm of my possibility. I simply set out to be a good lead engineer in my discipline." In his leadership classic, *On Becoming a Leader*, Warren Bennis describes that "people begin to become leaders at that moment when they decide for themselves how to be."[1] This requires learning along the way and collecting experiences and lessons and "transforming themselves into a new person." Bennis references Gib Akin of the McIntire School of Commerce, who describes various such modes of learning and one of the motivations of learning as "a person's perception of the gap between what he or she is, and what he or she should be." Paul fits this description perfectly.

It may be true that Paul did not have a specific plan, but his personality characteristics are such that he was eventually going to reach the point of asking himself, "What should I be?" We saw a similar question gnaw at Joseph Brewer in Chapter 6. Like the other leaders in our study, Paul is an engineer by training and therefore one would expect him to be like a hedgehog – a specialist with his nose to the ground,

---

[1] Warren Bennis, *On Becoming a Leader* (New York: Basic Books, 2009), 49.

oblivious of the horizon. But like our other successful leaders, Paul is a fox. Like so many others, after he had achieved
excellence in his domain, the foxy characteristics of being a
generalist and broadening one's horizons surfaced and so, after
spending five years becoming a good lead process engineer,
Paul asked himself, "What else should a good lead engineer
do that I have not yet done?" Asking the question is a manifestation of what Bennis calls *knowing thyself* and what Akin
refers to in one of his modes of learning.[2]

Paul began his leadership journey in the 1990s when he
started as a young process engineer working for an engineering design contractor, Brown and Root UK Ltd., with the
simple goal of being a good process engineer and eventually
becoming a lead process engineer. Having worked as a lead
process engineer, Paul wanted to put theory – designing the
processes and facilities for someone else – into practice by
actually being involved in a project during its execution. So,
Paul decided to join an operator and work in a commissioning
role.[3]

Commissioning is a multidisciplinary experience that
requires orchestrating the various disciplines of mechanical
and electrical engineering and instrumentation and control
along with the process engineering design knowledge to
ensure that a production facility will start up without major
issues and begin generating money for the owner. To start up
effectively, any capital projects that include process facilities
require the collaboration of multiple disciplines that often
don't speak the same technical language and teams that have
in many cases not been together for the entire length of the

---

[2] Ibid., 52–53.
[3] There is a lesson here for young leaders in that, just as Joseph Brewer, Don Vardeman,
Paul and others did, you have to chart your own path, not wait for it to be handed
down, and work the path one turn at a time.

project. This collaboration is not easy to achieve. It is not usually taught in engineering colleges, where the focus is on specialization in a discipline and not much focus is on learning of how other disciplines work. A leader's ability to work with multiple disciplines and to get all to work toward a common vision and future state becomes critically important and has been empirically validated time and again. Early exposure to such experiences stands out as one of the key contributors to a broadening of perspective, as we see from this and other leader profiles. As Paul said to us, "These were natural progressions for the journey of a process engineer and I got those opportunities early."

The next iteration of the question "What else should a good process engineer do that I have not yet done?" prompted Paul to find a role in the front-end development of a capital project. To do this he left his operating company to join a special front-end engineering consultancy, Genesis. "This provided some experience in short-term projects and studies and certainly benefited my presentation skills and report writing. We had quick turnarounds of projects and I had to deal with clients and get a message over and get it over quickly." Having done this for a while, the lure back to the engineering and pro-curement (E&P) side of the business and being involved in the bigger picture outside the single discipline was too great for Paul. Having gained a good reputation among his peers, he was approached to join Kerr-McGee as facilities engineer for a project they were executing in the UK. A combina-tion of project engineer and package manager, this involved a bit of project management, a bit of scheduling, and a bit of cost estimating. As he says, "packages are like mini-projects." Later, still with Kerr-McGee, he was given his first project as a project manager: "A nice-sized project with little bit of everything – engineering management, a brownfield program, a subsea program, construction, third-party infrastructure and integration."

Paul hasn't looked back since then and grabbed opportunities that came along "with both hands," leading up to his current position. Paul says, "All these opportunities did give me a feel for the role of planning and the understanding that you need a plan and work a plan to be successful." He is of course talking about projects, but those words also apply to strategically and thoughtfully developing young leaders by giving them curated opportunities.

For organizations looking to build a cadre of potential future project leaders, the focus has to be on underscoring for their young foxes the importance of being really competent at something fundamental/foundational first, and only then diversifying in other domains. Just as an architecturally beautiful building with transformative design or a mundane glass-and-steel office tower both start with similar foundational elements, without which both will be weak, so should a young engineer strive to be competent at something first. Understanding something basic – usually one's discipline – really well sets the foundational base upon which young engineers can layer a variety of experiences, lessons, and perspectives and transform themselves into what they want to be. Today, be it because of demographics or particular circumstances in an organization, we see many young professionals wanting to diversify too quickly.

It is also important to recognize that the times in which Paul was establishing his foundation and becoming competent, oil and gas companies still did retain many of the engineering competencies and talents in-house, which provided Paul with opportunities for growth. The outsourcing trend transformed that model, so that today owner companies rarely maintain in-house execution competencies. This often precludes opportunities to establish a solid disciplinary foundation. If future leaders require a successful foundation, then owner-company leaders need to think long and hard about whether they can honestly provide enough runway for young engineers to build that foundation.[4] That requires long-term thinking, which is in very short supply these days across the corporate world. Building an adequate supply of project leaders will therefore require the future leader and current chieftains of corporations to *know thyself.*

LITTLE BLACK BOOK

The analysis presented in Chapter 5 clearly showed how much successful leaders value and pay close attention to the people management part of their job. The leaders who are not very successful focus on technical, work process, and other procedural aspects. Further, we have seen in the profiles of all the leaders thus far that most of them had a specific group of people that they worked with on multiple projects and many followed the leader from one organization to the next. So how do you build a community of people that you can trust to deliver a successful project? The answer is deceptively simple, but one that requires foresight and a basic understanding of what drives project success. In Paul's case, it is a collector's diary. That diary collects experiences – success and failures – and specific individuals and their behaviors that led to the success. Paul described his method of learning as "my little black book."

The little black book contained something very important: the names of people Paul met along the way who were excellent contributors to project outcomes because they were self-motivated, competent, and got things done; their behaviors helped deliver a successful project. What is highly unusual,

---

[4] If owner organizations are not willing to help young prospective project leaders build the needed foundation, the young engineers will need to move from one owner or contractor to another to build the foundation for themselves.

but demonstrates foresight and a personality trait, is that relatively early in his career, Paul was already collecting names of people who could be good on a team if he ever was a project director. In fact, the first time Paul acted as project leader and needed people, he got his process engineer, safety engineer, subsea manager, construction manager, and installation manager by going back to his black book and finding those people. Paul is, in his own words, "a collector of people."

Being a collector of people doesn't distinguish Paul from every other successful project leader. What distinguishes Paul is that he started his collecting of people early and formalized the process so thoroughly in the little black book. In his collection process, Paul was looking for more than just competence. He was looking for people who are willing to go the extra mile because they have an intense desire to be successful and will work extremely hard. In fact, Paul admits that the people in his black book weren't always technically the best that were available, but they had great relationship behaviors and knew what needed to be done, how to work with each other, and therefore how to get things done. Most of all, they needed to care about the work they were doing. As he said, "Not everyone on the team needs to be a striker," to use the footballers term. Paul inherently knew what Chapter 5 proves, that emotional intelligence, trust, and relationships are critical to project success. Technical savvy alone is not enough. Paul learned early what some project managers never learn: people do projects, not the work process.

Paul was building what Peter Drucker called out as the chief object of leadership,[5] which is the creation of human community held together by the work bond for a common purpose. Consequently, the power of having a group of people whom

---

[5] Peter Drucker, *The Effective Executive* (New York: HarperCollins, 1967).

you trust to join such a community – a project team – cannot be overstated. However, this also means that to be able to get to a stage where you can collect such people requires that the foundational years not be shortened and plenty of diverse opportunities be made available. This is a difficult proposition and one not easily implementable without foresight and long-term focus.

The little black book did more than simply collect people. It also collected specific experiences and learnings that Paul had along the way. This was Paul's way of layering his disciplinary foundation with experience-based learning. Paul learned by doing and not only by reading. Just like any other successful leader, Paul has experienced failure as well as successes. The mark of good leaders is whether they can learn from the mistakes and failures and improve themselves for the next time. Paul says, "I would look back at a project and ask why something didn't work? What could I have done differently? I wouldn't do it this way again. Sometimes the issues that led to poor outcomes were technical and work related and sometimes they were simply poor behavior and relationship issues." All these experiences got neatly collected in the black book.

CATHARTIC PROJECT EXECUTION PLAN

Collecting lessons is nothing new to most project professionals. Yet we see again and again that lessons alone do not translate into successful projects. Almost every company with which we work has some form of extensive lessons-learned program. And yet, about two complex projects out of three fail, so lessons learned don't actually look like learned lessons. To effectively translate the lessons that he had so carefully recorded in the little black book, Paul Harris invented an actual mechanism for the translation: the cathartic project execution plan.

A project execution plan (PEP) is a document that is produced by almost all project teams in all of our clients across all industrial sectors. It is a ubiquitous document that is, in theory, supposed to tell the expected story of the project and its execution. Some of the PEPs we see are very good and some of the PEPs are utterly horrid. We have even seen entire PEPs copied and pasted in from other documents and teams have forgotten to even change the name of the original project. The PEPs rarely end up telling the story. In fact, in most companies the project leader rarely pens the execution strategy; more often than not the document is produced by multiple authors and ends up looking like a badly written movie where the scriptwriters cannot agree on the plot.

Paul's cathartic project execution plan stands in stark contrast. Paul always writes the execution plan and he would never read it after he had written it. It was his way of writing everything about how he thought the project should be executed and all the things he wanted to do differently on this project. That was his way, as he describes it, to get on paper his thoughts about project execution very early in the project. This is actually quite an ingenious way to learn because by writing on paper the execution strategy when the learnings from the previous project are fresh in your mind, you are forced to memorialize the practical impact of the learnings. The other benefit of Paul's ingenious strategy is that it allows him to develop a baseline plan that is unadulterated by other team members' views and yet allows the option to modify the baseline with new input. By writing the next execution plan, Paul is able to pull the learnings together from his little black book.

In fact, what Paul is doing is actually writing a success narrative for his project. He is saying, this is the way the project should go. Writing the execution plan is akin to writing the desired story of the project. How would I want the story of the project to read? Not unlike the scriptwriter of a movie, Paul is writing the story of the project with the focus on what scope needs to be included, what the execution strategy is, what resources are needed to support the strategy and the schedule. Cost is then output of all those things. And lastly, don't change the story. Optimize it, fine tune, but don't change the plot.

The PEP should be a culmination of all the bits and pieces of learning you have collected along the way. This of course means that a leader should be open to learning from anyone and everyone they come in contact with. That requires a personality that is open and inviting and also one that has an insatiable curiosity. As Paul says, "I am a magpie. I will steal good ideas from anybody and everybody." So as leaders progress through their careers, does this learning model change? Should it change? How should young leaders close their knowledge gaps as they progress through their careers and encounter larger projects with more diverse disciplines? Should a leader know everything about a project?

The cliché that leaders lead people and managers follow work process also holds true in how project leaders prepare themselves for new opportunities with bigger responsibilities. There is a lesson here for future leaders on why accepting responsibility for self-learning is a critical component of a leader's education. In *On Becoming a Leader*, Marty Kaplan describes accepting responsibility by describing how he created a self-designed university for himself to learn everything about the movie business so he could be successful as a VP of Disney productions.[6] Although he had a very diverse background and experiences, he had no exposure to the movie business and so he accepted the responsibility to educate himself on everything about movies.

Paul talks about a similar approach he uses when he first is assigned a new role. The first step is to understand the role he is going to take, map out his gaps, and then "try to fill my gaps" by finding the right people. Paul gives an example of when he was given his first role of a construction manager. Paul did not know much about construction management. But he knew himself and knew his gaps, so when he went to the yard for the first time as a construction manager he met the crew and workers and admitted to them that, "I don't know much about construction, but I have done other things in my life and I am willing to learn from you, if you are willing to teach me. I am here to get the job done successfully, to support you, to get you the tools you need, and to fight battles on your behalf." That again highlights the quality of openness but also shows that a leader is humble – not a shrinking violet – but humble, honest, and willing to accept responsibility to learn. When Paul was assigned to be a development manager – essentially managing the entire development including the subsurface – he took it upon himself to take subsurface courses, and asked for and spent one-on-one time with subsurface discipline leads to understand how seismic analysis is done, what a reservoir log analysis does, and how log data are interpreted. All this not to do their work, but rather so that he is knowledgeable enough in his role as a development manager and can appreciate and empathize with the discipline leads, and also ask intelligent questions.

---

[6] Bennis, On Becoming a Leader, 53–54.

Sadly, these qualities such as openness, willingness to recognize one's own blind spots, learning and understanding others' work are not qualities that are in abundance in leaders. The authors have encountered plenty of so-called leaders who have the title but express no desire to learn any discipline that's not theirs. As Paul says, "If I am going to run something, then I want to understand it deeply. If I am going to understand it deeply, then I want to learn about it. I sit down with my geologist and geophysicist and they explain the seismic lines to me and they see a reservoir and I see Mickey Mouse." But the reason to do this is so the people on the team know that when I ask them questions I have put in the effort to understand their work. Successful leaders focus on discovery and active learning, not on dogma, shock, or reactive learning.[7]

The discussion of leaders versus managers brings us to another key difference between the two. As Bennis suggests,[8] managers focus on systems, structures, and processes while leaders focus on people. Paul's focus on people and his approach to long-term relationships with people has to be one of the central plots in his story of success. In fact, many of the key people Paul has worked with were people he met when he was a young graduate. They were senior technical people who were higher in seniority than Paul. But they stayed technical and were happy to teach Paul everything they knew just as Paul was eager to learn everything they knew. Eventually Paul was their peer and soon thereafter their boss. Of course, the strong relationship they forged was helpful when they were working for Paul. Success is drawn out from these people in the way they are involved in all aspects of projects and they are given the freedom to set up their discipline teams in any

---

[7] Bennis, *On Becoming a Leader*, 69.
[8] Ibid., 42.

way they wish as long as it achieves the vision of the project. In fact, as Paul says, almost none of the projects that he leads has ever had a formal interface manager role. A role that is so common in the industry in most companies is a role that he does not have mostly because a "construction manager and his team are responsible for everything to do with construction, including everyone and everything that they will touch, and the engineering manager is responsible for everything and everyone the engineering team will interface with."[9]

The leader's job is then to set the vision, set up the team with a right combination of skills, behaviors, and personalities, and let it run organically rather than through mandate. The self-awareness that leaders display also shows through in Paul's approach to staffing his team (and asking for his leads to do the same) with someone with background and personalities that can cover for his blind spot. The same approach to people carries over to Paul's philosophy of dealing with contractors.

The difference between a project leader and project manager becomes obvious when one contrasts their approaches toward contractors. Most project managers use the systems, structures, rules, and contracts as a way to manage the relationship. Paul has approached this critical relationship by building trust by asking each contractor about to receive the bid, "Why should we give you the award?" Often the difference between the winner and second place has been their response to this question, which provides an insight into how they approach relationship building. After the award, Paul routinely visits each location to meet every person working on his project to build trust and a one-to-one connection. (Paul proudly stated that on one of the last projects he did as a project leader he knew 95% of the 200-plus people on the management level

---

[9] This approach to interface management is similar to the one described by Jay Sexton.

of the entire project team.) The philosophy embodied in here is that "you do not want to have the first conversation with people or contractors when there is a problem."

Throughout his career Paul has been willing to take on opportunities and challenges in order to gain experiences, even though some of them may not have ended up as the most successful. Nevertheless, the experience makes you better. No one likes difficult situations but the more you are exposed to them the more comfortable you become. A young engineer or a young leader may be willing to take on such opportunities, but the other ingredient that is necessary is a mentor. Mentors spotted something in Paul, pushed him hard, and gave him opportunities that were "quite frankly above the level" he could do for his age, experience, and knowledge, but they challenged him and he didn't want to disappoint. Paul added, "I still believe in the old mantra that you have to protect your boss, not let them down or give them surprises." The capital industries we deal with today are sorely deficient in strong mentorship programs. Most companies have some sort of formal mentorships or many of the readers may even be involved in some mentoring programs, but sadly many of these programs don't seem to produce a cadre of strong potential leaders. In fact, many of the leaders we interviewed for this book agreed that most corporate mentorship programs don't work as effectively as on-the-job mentoring that is based on a mutual trust and deep working relationship and a coach–student model. Paul had technical professionals along the way who took Paul as their subject to mold. Paul's mentors started out as senior to him in positions when Paul started, then they were Paul's peers and then the mentors were junior in rank to Paul, but the coaching continued because it was based on trust and a long-term working relationship. If we as an industry are going to succeed in the future, we must create opportunities for young leaders where such natural coaching can germinate and thrive, mentors who will step up to look after young leaders and coach them for a long term because they see something in the young leader, not because its required.

So, what is a great project leader? What is exemplary project leadership? Is it possible to define exemplary leadership? Maybe you can only define it at the end of a project. But then, it is surely easier to say that someone was a great project leader if the project delivered superior cost or schedule outcomes. What if the project does not deliver the results but the project leader still did everything right? Paul defines exemplary leadership as "when the team wants to work for you again." And the first few ingredients necessary to achieve that result are competence (be good at something first), know thyself (self-awareness), and be a magpie (be open to other people's views and learn from others), and most importantly build a collection of trusted people and learnings, not a collection of processes.

At the start of this chapter we quoted Paul Harris describing himself as a magpie. In folklore magpies are known as thieves that collect shiny objects. Paul Harris is a collector as well. He collects people who shine and lessons that are learned. A magpie indeed!

CHAPTER 11
DAVID YOUNG

People Do Projects

In February 2017 we had just wrapped up an engagement for a long-time client of ours and were enjoying a nice lunch discussing the leadership research that led to this book. As we discussed the characteristics of successful leaders, one person at the table inquired if we had interviewed David Young for our profiles. "You've got to interview David Young if you are going to talk about successful project leaders!" was the response we got when we said that we hadn't interviewed him. We found out at the same lunch, however, that David Young had already been retired from this company for about a year and a half at the time. Well, we tracked him down and he graciously agreed to sit down with us and provide his perspective on project leadership.

David Young has combined an analytical approach to project leadership with a high degree of emotional intelligence to produce an approach to managing complex projects that led to a very successful track record and whose aura still lingers in the halls of the company he worked for, even in his retirement.

We started our discussions with David describing his view of the role of a project leader. David explained that the "leadership [role] changes with time. If a project is big and complex, it can only be delivered by many people working together in concert, across many time zones, in many different companies. Leadership is about conducting that orchestra so that it is in tune, it is on the same beat, and it is consistent with what the audience expects. So that's the same way if it's a big project or a small project. But the leader needs to work out whether it's a quartet or a jazz band or a full concert orchestra that is the project, and act appropriately."

The uncanny part about this view of leadership is that it matches exactly with our view of leadership as discussed in Chapter 3. Yet, David expressed his views almost 12,000 miles apart from us, to a colleague of ours. Of course, David is exactly right. Project leadership is about conducting an orchestra of various members who may or may not have worked together before and ensuring that dynamic works well even though each person, each player, may be a good solo artist. It is said that the life of an orchestra conductor is nomadic. While not necessarily nomadic in the true sense of the word, David has had a nomadic journey gaining a very diverse background and experiences that have certainly played a large role in shaping his approach to, and areas of focus in, project leadership.

David grew up on a farm in the United Kingdom. His father and his grandfather were farmers. David believes that growing up on a farm where his father and grandfather worked made a big difference in his personality, "because you know what your dad does, he doesn't *go to* work but he's *at work* when he's home and there was no distinction between work and pleasure." David believes that the childhood experience of seeing his father and grandfather work on the farm, which was home, is why he carries a sense of enjoyment in work, rather than a sense of pain or frustration. David's other grandfather was a project manager and instilled in him a love for projects and diverse global experiences. As a project manager, his grandfather traveled the world building factories to blow glass bottles. He would leave England with a set of plans, a "circular electric credit on boat" (a round-trip ticket by boat for unspecified times), and would come back two or three years later having built and commissioned bottle plants in New Zealand, Australia, South Africa, and South America. David recalls "long conversations when [I] was young about how he saw life on his travels and how projects were so exciting."

David completed the usual schooling and graduated with a degree in chemical engineering, which is not uncommon in the leaders we surveyed. However, after graduating with an engineering degree, David wasn't particularly interested in going to work. Upon some coaxing from his father, who gave David an advertisement for a job, he joined a Panamanian registered company and immediately started traveling the world for them. While this wasn't a chemical engineering role per se, David used his engineering background and education as a stepping-stone into the world of oil and gas. This Panamanian company would work wherever major oil and gas companies didn't want to do the work themselves and so as a young graduate, shaped by his family to love work and travel the world, David traveled to South America, North America, India, and the Persian Gulf doing work for oil and gas companies. David worked on his very first liquefied natural gas (LNG) plant, working for this Panamanian company on Das Island, Abu Dhabi.

After traveling the world for a while, doing projects all over the world, David decided to work onshore in London to settle down. That turned out to be a short-lived plan as his company sent him off to the Republic of Ireland to start a new company. The assignment was to design and develop the installation of the Ninian platform in the North Sea working on grouting installation as a subcontractor. David's early jobs were different than most of our other successful leaders in that he did everything except what he was trained to do. Grouting wells in the North Sea is not the usual young chemical engineer's path. What is typical is that he did lots of different things in his early years that became his "developmental experiences," as David puts it.

Developmental experiences are those experiences that one must have to be a complete _____ (fill in the blank). In other words, if you haven't had those experiences, you are probably missing something in the journey to become complete in something. What developmental experiences are necessary to become a good doctor, a good pilot, or a good platoon leader? What developmental experiences are necessary to become a successful complex project leader? Researchers have found that for experiences to be developmental, they have to provide a crucible for the leader to grow. They have to be high impact and challenging experiences that often present a "crisis of personal limitations." The necessary ingredient in a developmental experience is the presence of self-awareness – that is, a sense of one's personal strengths and weaknesses and the willingness to confront reality. Other components of developmental experiences are feedback, support, and growth.[1]

David's early developmental experience was working with and managing people and this shaped his entire approach to project leadership. Describing his experiences working for the Panamanian contractor David explained that, "[he] always enjoyed the creation phase more than the amass phase, the building thing rather than the designing thing." And as part of

---

[1] Developmental experiences as defined, described, and attributed in *From Battlefield to Oilfield,* which Nate Self presented to the IPA Upstream Industry Benchmarking Consortium annual meeting, 13–15 November 2017.

this building phase, David and his company used crews from all over the world to build their projects. David worked with construction crews made up of people from South Africa or from the Dominican Republic or any number of other countries that provided the labor. The crews from South Africa spoke some English but many others didn't. Everyone, including David, had to learn about the reality of working with human beings with different backgrounds and cultures, on the job, in the middle of construction. The reasons this was a developmental experience was because David had to manage people – construction crews – at a very early age. Although there was support from other people around him, he had to confront his own weaknesses and grow through this experience. He had to understand how people thought and responded to him as a fresh graduate and then over time as a mature engineer. But coming out of this experience, David quickly learned the reality that if you are doing a big complex project, you have to do it with a lot of people and that means you have to understand how each person thinks (we will describe a more specific example a bit later in the chapter). His early childhood and early career experiences shaped David's views of work: you have to love your work, people are the essence of the work, and you can't run complex projects sitting behind the desk.

As we discussed in Chapter 4, very few of the leaders we surveyed for this book actually started their careers as project leaders. Similarly, David started his journey working for the contractor side of projects and then took several interesting "developmental" stops along his journey toward becoming a project leader. After spending his early career working for the Panamanian company, David got married, bought a house, and before starting a family he and his wife decided to travel since his wife had never traveled before. David and his wife decided to "find somebody who will pay us to come over to Australia." Well someone did and so David and his wife moved to Australia where David spent about two years in a project management role in the mining industry in Northwest Australia.

After two years in the mining environment, David took a job with a consultancy based in Perth, Australia. The consultancy did a lot of work for Woodside Energy and after seeing David's work firsthand, Woodside tapped him on the shoulder for a special assignment. Woodside and the state government of Western Australia needed someone to create (from scratch) regulations for an onshore LNG plant because there were no regulations at that point in time for that sort of environment. As David remembers it, he was told that it had been agreed between Woodside and four different government agencies that he would be the ideal candidate for this job. "As I had been a consultant for a while, I had been around and got known to various people. They said, ring the director-general of the Department of Mines and Energy and you will get the job," is how David describes his job interview.

So in the late 1980s, David spent four years working for the state regulator but also interacting with the federal government and industry players to put onshore LNG regulations in place. In the early 1990s, after four years with the state regulator, David "literally walked across the street to the Woodside offices" where they offered him a job. That is how he started the second phase of his project leadership journey. However, even after joining Woodside with significant experience, he was rotated through various departments in a true apprenticeship model. David worked in health and safety, then as chief safety engineer in the chemical engineering department, and then as a project engineer responsible for Floating Production Storage and Offloading (FPSO) design before finally moving,

formally, into a project management role, which he retired
from after 25 successful years in 2015.

As the readers can surmise, prior to joining Woodside,
David had already amassed almost a decade's worth of varied
experience. This is a commonality we have seen in all the
leaders we have profiled. David's path to project leadership
was more thoroughly generalist than most. His developmental
experiences were unusually eclectic and nonlinear. He is a
true fox who skipped the more typical hedgehog step in his
career development. But he was able to bring together his
numerous sources of knowledge and experiences to tackle
the next challenge. That is how he was able to successfully
move from working for a contractor to project management
in the mining industry to writing LNG regulations for a state
regulator. Even highly skilled specialists – hedgehogs – who
have become highly skilled through a mechanistic way
would struggle to learn something new organically. Surely,
David's generalist personality helped him through a varied
background, but it is also the experiences he got that allowed
the generalist to thrive further.

The strong generalist personality that is at the core of
David's success is further highlighted in the way David
explains his view of an ideal project leader. "Partly intuition!"
That is how David initially responds to the question of how
he selects future project leaders or people who work on his
team. Being the analytical type, David expounds by discussing
the other elements he considers when selecting future leaders.
"Let me talk about the things that you could measure," he
says. "If an individual takes things personally, they shouldn't
be a project leader. If an individual can't differentiate between
people doing their best and people being successful, they
shouldn't be a project leader. What that means is that a good
project leader sets up people to be successful and dimensions

their tasks so that if they are operating at a 5% stretch of their capabilities [and if all others are doing the same], the project would be a success. If you blame individuals for not being successful but you have designed their tasks [beyond the 5% or so stretch] that they are beyond anything that they have ever done before or what's been achieved, you can't blame them."

Through his experiences, David has come to his own model of selecting people based on their characteristics and how those characteristics fit the project context. As we discussed in Chapter 1, most organizations don't have a selection model, let alone one that accounts for individual characteristics and matches them with project situations. David, while labeling what he does as intuition, has actually been relying on characteristics, which this research proves is what determines success. "The other dimension that I look for in all my subproject managers is that they don't make assumptions. People who make assumptions are not good managers. Project management is about "I don't know, but I will find out." In other words, generalists, who don't know all subjects but know a little bit of a lot of things and know how to find solutions. An essential part of a project leader's toolkit is the ability to know enough of each subject to ask very intelligent questions. That is how a generalist functions. This is very similar to what Paul Harris did in understanding seismic analysis and other technical details, just enough to ask intelligent questions.

The last element in David's model for selecting project managers is enthusiasm.[2] He says, "There has to be enthusiasm because it's hard work and sometimes mind numbingly hard work. It's not hard because of the burden; it's got to do with

---

[2] Recall from Chapter 4 that the optimism dimension on the Five-Factor Model was characteristic of successful project leaders.

the various elements of complexity of the project and where each element could be on a particular day."[3]

In Chapter 5, Figure 5.1, we provided a causal link of how a project leader's personality and characteristics translate into good or bad project outcomes. The core element of this causal pathway is the tasks that the project leaders choose to perform – or rather, the tasks that the project leader chooses to spend more time on or thinks are more important than other tasks. Chapter 5 also highlighted that leaders who spend more time on people (including contractors and vendors) management, communication, and stakeholder management tend to be more successful. We have already seen how David's personality traits, background, and experience match quite closely with the research and with other leaders. But we wanted to deeply understand the tasks David performs, tasks he considered critical, and his approach to those tasks to see the causal pathway in action.

PEOPLE MANAGEMENT

We started our discussion with David's approach to people management and specifically building a project organization. Building the right team is of great importance to David because of his intense focus on a people-centered approach to project management by setting up people to deliver a successful project and not depending on processes or other mechanistic tools for success.

David's approach to project-team organization and structure depends on how long the project is estimated to take and

---

[3] Project professionals are a special breed. Given the long timelines, multiple work fronts and locations that people work in, number of daily decisions that have to be made, and all other pressures, people who work projects have to, must, really enjoy projects – the creation and building of something – to endure the hard work.

on the number of managers he needs. He approaches the organization analytically as well. For instance, on the last project
David and his management team decided to study various
historical projects and their organizations before deciding on
the organization structure for their project. David's guiding
principle is to create structures that actually require scope
managers to work with each other and in fact rely on each
other for the success of the project. In a sense, what we are
seeing here is a different way to implement the shared success
and shared leadership model we read about in the chapters of
Joseph Brewer and Don Vardeman. After studying the historical models, the one that David adopted involved managers
working across various streams – design, procurement,
fabrication, construction, installation – of a specific scope in a
larger project. But those managers knew that sometime in the
future they would then become the engineering manager, or
the procurement manager, or the fabrication manager for all
the scopes – so essentially they were managing vertically for
the entire project. That meant that the managers knew they
had to rely on each other and it also meant that during the
early phase of the project they had to work to set things up
for their own and others' success. That is indeed an ingenious
way to drive shared leadership and shared success down in the
organization.[4] Of course, this model can work for complex
projects with many scopes that have long durations, but the
model will fall flat if implemented on a very fast-paced project,
for instance. That means that one must first fully understand

---

[4] This reminds Neeraj of a course he took during his MBA program. One of the pro-
fessors had set up a similar way to grade course work done by a team – so a team
project – as opposed to individual submission. The grades for the team project were
based on the project itself but also considered how each team member rated the other
members, anonymously, for their contribution to the project. The goal was to encourage all members to contribute and pull their own weight.

the context and complexity of the project at hand before working on the organizational aspect of managing the project.

The other critical element that such a model needs to succeed is that most of the managers of the scopes need to be generalists themselves. In other words, if they have been a specialist manager all their life (a leader of specialists) say for pipeline, or topsides, or subsea scope, it is unlikely that they can perform the scope manager role in the way David builds the organization. David is essentially deploying leaders of scope and he is acting as the leader of leaders. Such an approach to organization is critical because, as David recognizes, a successful project is successful only because the entire project team is sharing the risks and successes equally, which helps them drive toward a common goal. That is a leader's job after all. Any group that is measured on its own success that sits within a project will try to minimize only *their* risks to the detriment of the project if their success isn't linked to project success. The same issue manifests in other parts of the larger oil and gas organizations. For example, the reason the oil and gas industry hasn't systematically been able to embrace standardization is because of different groups being measured differently, which in and of itself isn't unusual, but a lack of leadership such as David's makes bringing together different groups of people nearly impossible.

COMMUNICATION

Having worked for contractors before joining an owner firm, David has a good deal of empathy for contractors and his approach to people management extends to creating a shared success structure for the entire supply chain rather than the owner alone. A philosophy that David shares with every other successful project leader interviewed is that success cannot be

viewed as zero-sum. The goal for our leaders is that every individual and organization associated with their projects will feel
the pride of success at the end of the day. The contributions
of all will be acknowledged and those contributions will be
rewarded by admission to the next project whenever possible.

However, David, like the others, also believes that neither
the contractors nor the owners should carry all the risks and
that frank conversations early are needed to understand what
constitutes success and failure for each party and to understand what kinds of risks they feel secure in taking and what
kinds of risks they do not feel they can bear. This approach is
far better than finding out later that the risks assigned to the
contractor are beyond what they can cope with. What comes
through repeatedly is the necessity to treat everyone involved
with respect.

David provides an example of when he set up an owner's
forum for a project of his. The owner's forum comprised
owners – CEO level – and representatives of each of the
operator, supplier, contractor, and vendor organizations
involved in the project. The idea for this forum came from
David reaching out to another oil and gas operator who was
willing to hear and try out new ideas. A three-day workshop
was organized with all the owners of the various entities
involved in the project, at a very expensive venue (to show the
seriousness of the effort), to end up with a charter – a shared
charter – among all the participating companies, contractors
included, that laid out the vision for shared success. One of the
shared success elements in the charter was, "I will not surprise
any of the parties involved, which means other contractors as
well as the client, with any late information." Simple words
with power to save tens of millions of dollars, created through
a workshop that David discovered by being open to others'
ideas. The workshop did in fact save millions of dollars.

During the installation phase of the project above, various installation contractors started sharing installation and transport vessels with each other to help ensure each contractor's scope was well executed. Although this wasn't part of the contract, they had pledged to a shared success charter. Additionally, during this time, one of the insulated flowlines on the project was cracking, so they had to make a new flowline, which led to a three-month delay. During this delay, the transportation and installation vessels used the time to get ready for the installation. However, the only company that got paid anything was the flowline company for the second line. The contractors did not charge standby time, as is the norm, because of the commitment to shared success.[5]

Getting people to believe in your shared success vision, getting them to follow your lead requires, at the end of the day, a level of trust. The followers have to feel that you are honest and they can put their faith and trust in you. That is dependent on communication. How well does the leader communicate and interact with the people he wishes to follow his lead to engender their trust in him? Information is the lifeblood of any project, but much more so for large complex projects in which the supply chain is usually globally dispersed. How do leaders like David ensure that people — team members, suppliers, contractors — trust them to always provide them true and accurate information?

---

[5] The story of this particular project sounds very much like how alliancing project contracts are supposed to work, but almost never do. The reason so many of the alliancing arrangements fail is because they miss the essential ingredient: the development of shared goals, mission, and trust. Too often, those putting the alliance contract together believe that a contract — a document — can substitute for the hard, honest work of getting to know the contractors and vendors as people, understanding their concerns, and treating them with respect.

We asked David his take on the often-heard view from
many project teams that contractors don't always provide a
true status report on project progress until it is too late, which
has led to some fraying in owner/contractor relationships.[6]
David was emphatic in disagreeing with that view, saying,
"No, actually they don't do that!" He went on to say, "You
have to understand the national characteristics and culture and
upbringing of the contractor's project manager and commer-
cial/contracts manager. If you are a Westerner working in Sin-
gapore or Indonesia or Korea, the way you would behave with
a Western operator would be different than if you are a local."
David explains a recent example of how he approached the
issue of building trust. "We have to start by doing research
to understand the people we will be working with. On our
last job, in Korea, I got one of our Korean employees in our
company to spend time with me explaining to me the history of Korea. I have a whole set of notes going back the
last 5,000 years of Korean history. So after we awarded the
contract and took the Korean management team to dinner, I
could really understand and respect the individuals at a personal level. I understood what it meant if they were the eldest
son or daughter, whether they had family records. This is how
I could build trust with individuals. So if and when problems
do arise in execution, this trust ensures that the news does
reach me. You will be told what is going on, honestly. But
you have to work very hard and long at that." Albeit a lot
more analytical in terms of the research David did, you will
recall that this is a similar habit that Paul Harris had when he
would be at a point of awarding contracts; he would interview
each contractor and after giving the award he would ensure
that he knew every person on the contractor's team.

---

[6] Actually, it more often leads to something approximating brain-stem hatred.

STAKEHOLDER MANAGEMENT

Complex projects come with a complex set of stakeholders who all need to be managed. There are many stakeholders on a team. They each have the power – and often an itch to wield that power – which means that they have to be managed. As we saw in Chapter 4, stakeholder management is a task that's considered important by successful managers. This should, of course, be no surprise. Heaven help the project leader who knowingly ignores stakeholder management! But all the leaders we surveyed for the research also indicated that they do not consider stakeholder management to be a value-adding task. It is necessary, but not value adding. These seemingly incongruous results are because stakeholder management has turned into less of conversations and more of reporting – reports for internal sponsors, reports for joint-venture partners, and reports to government agencies – and it is the constant reporting that leaders consider nonvalue adding. David describes his methods of managing all these stakeholders.

First, the project managers on his team – his direct reports – are managed via the monthly report. Most, if not all, project teams generate a monthly report to provide a progress update on the project. Call us cynical, but generally speaking these monthly reports are a copy/paste job and usually they are outdated the day they come out because on a large complex project by the time the information is gathered to update the month's progress, the project has already moved on. Nevertheless, every team does this religiously and, as we say in Chapter 4, a project leader spending time on controls, of which the monthly report is a part, isn't very beneficial. But David uses it quite ingeniously.

While most of the industry is moving toward some sort of automated monthly reports, or dashboard-heavy monthly reports, David has firmly held against that trend. He mandates his project managers to write monthly reports in plain English to tell the story of the project at its current state. They are, in some ways, not allowed to simply report labor hours, or progress curves, or pictures. The goal is to tell a story and for each manager to then understand the story of the other parts of the project. So, while they may each be directing a scene, by reading the monthly reports, they can put the movie together and help other managers at any approaching nodes. David readily admits to having his managers cumulatively spend, in total, close to two years on reports on large complex projects. The key insight here is that telling a story is a completely different mental exercise than filling out a monthly report. Crafting a story requires that one consider how to start, what information helps develop the narrative, and finally how to wrap the story up so that it is satisfying to both writer and reader.

For external stakeholders such as joint-venture partners or other entities, David would provide dashboards from the monthly reports in the owner meetings but would encourage ideas and seek help if any of the joint-venture partners' technical representatives had experiences or solutions for specific issues the project is facing. By being inclusive and being open to help, he would convert them into not just a stakeholder on the sidelines but also a member of the team.

For internal stakeholders, David said that he used the organizational bureaucracy to help him. If internal stakeholders did not cooperate, then "I engaged whoever was my sponsor in terms of the project for that part of the organization and escalated. The bureaucracy is there to help me. Sometimes it doesn't feel that way but if you can understand their needs, then you can understand that you are going to have to put up with the person." Being someone who doesn't like leaving things to chance, David actually carried around a whitepaper on characteristics of good project sponsors that he used in his opening conversation with every new sponsor. The goal of using this paper was to create a structure for a successful and helpful relationship between the sponsor – a key internal stakeholder – and David. "For instance, I would promise that I'm not going to surprise you, I'm going to keep you well informed, [but] I need your time. I need you to stop conversations going in the wrong direction in meetings that I don't attend. I want you to maintain the good reputation of [my] project team and the project through good times and bad."[7]

We hope that by now the readers have picked up the similarities across all the leader profiles. For instance, the similarity between David's owner's forum and Don's relationship-based approach to contracting. The similarity between David's philosophy of how project management is not done sitting at a desk and Nora'in's philosophy of leaving the office and visiting people at their workplace. The similarity between Joseph's approach to learning from industry best practices – his plumb line – and David's analytical approach to studying what others have done in historical projects. There are similarities between Paul's cathartic execution plan, which is where he writes the story of the project for himself, and David's use of monthly story reports. Jay's approach to carefully and methodically building a project team would resonate with Dzul and David in the way they purposefully select a diverse set of people and structure the teams.

However, we also hope that the readers have picked up on how uncanny it is that seven successful complex project

---

[7] This ability to cultivate and then use network ties is one of the common characteristics of successful complex project leaders. This requires high emotional intelligence and is one of the key products of a project leader's experience within his or her company. Every complex project leader needs allies.

leaders across the globe from six different companies, who grew up in different times, with different cultural backgrounds, all display almost exactly the same habits and professional upbringing, which is tied to very similar personalities across all of them. This is strong evidence that the research presented in Part I of this book isn't just theory but is precisely what works in practice. Further, this also means that we *can* select project leaders for precisely the characteristics we seek, to engender the right tasks and habits, to lead a group of highly skilled professionals toward a common goal. In the next chapter, we will conclude our discussion by reviewing what we have learned and applying those learnings to better complex project leader selection in the future.

CHAPTER 12

WHAT HAVE WE LEARNED AND WHAT DOES IT MEAN?

We suspect that much – perhaps all – of what we have learned will be entirely obvious to excellent project leaders. However, given how small that population is there will likely be some important learnings for most readers. We will start this concluding section by discussing the key things that we can now prove quantitatively that were known only anecdotally before. There are also some important lessons from our interviews with successful project leaders to share. We hope all these lessons will be picked up by those who aspire to lead complex projects in the future. We will then draw the implications for the companies and agencies around the world that sponsor large complex projects. We complete this section by addressing a set of practical how-to questions that we believe senior corporate and business executives charged with selecting leaders for their complex projects will want answered.

WHAT WE HAVE LEARNED

1. Selecting the right project leader is important to project outcomes. The analysis in Chapters 4 and 5 proves that characteristics other than just being a smart, well-trained, and experienced project manager are essential for complex project success. This point may seem entirely obvious to some, but it clearly has not been obvious to those

charged with putting the right people into complex project leadership positions because they have not been making very good choices. Twelve large industrial companies nominated project leaders to answer our questions. We could find consistency in project leader selection in only one of those companies and, unfortunately, their selection criteria were systematically wrong and their dismal track record on complex projects is a result of those errors. Recall from our survey reported in Chapter 1 that only two of 49 respondents even mentioned personality among the characteristics considered in leader selection.

2. Our successful complex project leaders are all engineers by basic training and they share many personality traits that are common of engineers: conscientiousness, emotional stability, and extraversion. But they are very different from their colleagues in several key dimensions. They are much more open as measured by the Five-Factor Model. They also score uniformly higher on almost every dimension of the Emotional Intelligence Scale. They are generalists by nature who found the constraints associated with working inside their particular engineering discipline too confining. However, when they did work within their original engineering disciplines early in their careers, they were very good at what they did. The project management path was not chosen due to original failure.

3. The successful leaders were much more likely to have broader employment backgrounds than the less successful. They were more likely to have started with another company and often in another industry. Many came to project management by accident rather than design. There was only one element of their careers within their companies that appeared to make them better leaders:

a stint as a liaison on one or more projects operated by other companies. It appears that successful leaders, whose openness makes them good learners, benefited greatly by watching others do complex projects. Interestingly, working as a non–project leader on their own company's projects did not seem to have the same beneficial effect as being a liaison to a nonoperated project. We speculate that seeing another company's culture and working in a critic's role opened a lot of eyes to new possibilities.

4. Project practices, such as complete owner team integration and front-end loading, remain important, but they must be seen within the context of strong leadership and not in isolation. Strong teams are forged by strong leaders. Indeed, we found in our interviews that some effective leaders have their own staffing models and do their own team recruiting, some even from outside the company. Strong teams in turn get the right practices completed in the right order at the right time. Following the company's practices and work processes by rote without the full team alignment and strong leadership does not produce the desired result.

5. In fact, the effective project leaders do not spend much of their own time on work process. They chose to spend their time on people management, alignment, and communication to all including the contractors. It's not that they have disdain for work process, controls and other project management tasks, and technical work in general, they just do not consider those things *their* work. Remember, most of our successful project leaders were very good at technical tasks early in their careers, so it is not the case that they do not value such work. We also found that when project leaders do focus on things that belong to others, they were much less likely to have all needed functions on board for the project. We could find

no evidence that this was because they were understaffed on the project.

6. One characteristic of strong leaders is they make decisions. They do not feel comfortable delegating decision making to others. Guarding decision-making authority, of course, renders them fully accountable for results. There is no group-think, no striving for consensus, and no going along to be a good sport. They listen to others but make their own decisions. It is vitally important to understand, however, that they do not make decisions that belong to others. The successful leaders delegated project management work on their complex project to their project managers. Because they had spent a good deal of time early in projects getting to know the strengths and weaknesses of those working for them, they knew when to trust them to make the right decisions within their domain.

7. Most of those whom we interviewed had developed their own unique learning model. What was most remarkable is they were very aware of their learning model. It was operating in the foreground, not the background. Five of the seven interviewed volunteered information about their personal learning model and *not a single one mentioned their company's approved lessons-learned system.* Being a careful and systematic learner is perhaps the single most important characteristic to identify in a candidate for complex project leadership. A high degree of openness in their personalities as measured on the Five-Factor Model sets the stage for lifelong learning. Most of those whom we interviewed were toward the final third of their careers or more. But their learning model was just as active as it had ever been. There was no sense whatever of "I've been there and I know it all."

8. Most successful complex project leaders prefer to select their core team themselves and some have a very complete staffing model. Two of those interviewed even maintain their own talent pool. This is not at all surprising, but it is a message to functionally-based and weak matrix systems that they need to modify their approaches to team staffing. Many of our clients struggle to identify effective staffing models for their projects. Some put far too many owner people on the project who tend to generate work rather than get work done. Some staff too thinly and don't provide the project leader with enough muscle and brainpower to control the project. But those struggling to find the right staffing model might do well to ask their successful complex project leaders how *they* would staff a project.

9. The successful leaders all mentioned informal mentors they had learned from along the way. They all seemed to us to be deeply grateful for the time and interest that their informal mentors had granted them. Saying "thank you" and meaning it seems to be one of their common traits. All those interviewed had selected their own mentors; no one mentioned a mentor who had been assigned to them. Some of the mentors were their bosses and some worked outside their line altogether, but all were self-selected. We believe the lesson here is simple: learners find mentors. Organizations should focus their mentoring programs on those for whom learning is not easy or internally self-organized.

WHAT DOES IT MEAN?

We have to conclude that the process by which companies, agencies, and other sponsors select leaders for their most important projects is not working. The usual model is to offer progressively larger and more complex projects to project managers until they fail and that suffices as a career path – an application of the *Peter Principle*. We believe that project size is usually used as the proxy for complexity, but that often does not suffice. Skilled project managers who work in a transactional fashion without regard for the people side of projects will succeed up to some level of complexity and then will fail completely in their first genuinely complex project.

When Is a Project Complex?

Understanding the point at which a project becomes complex is essential to making the right choice of project leaders. Of course, it isn't really a point but a zone in which the three elements of complexity – scope, organization, and shaping – transform a straightforward project into a complex project. We have not yet quantified the level of complexity at which transactional project management becomes an immediate danger to projects, but there are some key indicators of complexity:

- When the number of subprojects is large enough that a real organizational center is required, the level of complexity is too high for transactional leadership (if one can even use that term).
- If the project is viewed as systemically critical to the sponsor organization's health or survival, then the project is inherently political internally and should be treated as complex.
- If there are determined opponents of the project with the means to disrupt, the project is complex.

- If the alignment of internal or external stakeholders will continue to be an active problem through execution, the project needs a real leader with vision and alignment skills.
- If the project is large and must be schedule-driven to achieve value, then the project should be treated as complex.[1]

Developing Future Project Leaders

In the past we at IPA believed that the primary problem for complex project leadership was that very few leaders had prior experience with a project of similar difficulty. The current study calls that belief into doubt. There were a number of project leaders who were successful with their first complex megaproject. A number of our interviewees succeeded with every complex project they have attempted. Of course, there are very few project directors with a series of failures, but there are some. We know of one who had the dubious distinction of leading disastrous projects on four continents before he was finally removed permanently!

The right experience appears to consist first of early success in the future leader's chosen technical discipline. We believe this establishes credibility of the person later when supervising those doing technical work but no longer doing such work themselves. This is one of several reasons why we believe that it would be quite difficult for a nontechnically trained

---

[1] Most large projects that place highest value on schedule and establish a difficult to achieve schedule target are not actually driven to that strategy by value. More often they are driven to that strategy by internal competition for capital or by a deadly game that businesses sometimes play with the project's organization, in which the business believes that "if I tell them 33 months, they'll take 36 but if I tell them 30 months they'll take 33." Schedule-driven to achieve value means that the requirements of the market require a schedule that is shorter than industry average.

person to take on project leadership even if they otherwise had the needed leadership qualities. The early disciplinary success also establishes the value and importance of such work in the future project leader.

What should the career path look like for the successful complex project leader? The early career development should start quite conventionally with the young engineer demonstrating that he or she can master work within their discipline. The mastery of that first discipline provides the foundation for success and that first acceptance by one's peers that one is a strong player. Those who express a desire for broader horizons on the technical side of the company should be tested for the personality traits and emotional intelligence that would suggest they can become complex project leaders. Those with the needed traits should be encouraged to broaden their experience, but with the following caveat. The kind of development-assignment stints that high fliers are given in companies do not appear to work for our project leaders. The development assignments suffer from being too short, too contrived, and often without closure as the high potential person is moved to an assignment that is already in progress and often moved out before lessons can be learned and internalized. Most of the assignments that developed the successful project leaders were assignments that they requested and that they saw through to completion.

Our most successful project leaders all seem to have been exposed to complexity in one form or another early in their careers. They had learned the importance of working out of difficult situations with people savvy, not just technical savvy alone. For companies that have a number of joint venture projects, we would strongly encourage putting the developing complex project leader into a liaison position on at least one such project.

Mentoring programs don't appear to have had much role in the development of successful complex project leaders. Based on our interviews, we believe that emotionally intelligent people seek out and secure their own mentors and neither need nor benefit from appointed mentors. Similarly, and this is an old finding, formal lessons-learned programs are not nearly as important as the individual's own model of learning. When trying to orchestrate the development of complex project leaders, explore whether the candidates have developed a learning model for themselves. If they have not, encourage them to do so.

Finally, when you find and develop a person and believe he or she is ready to lead their first complex project, install them in the leadership position just as early as possible in the lifecycle of the project. These successful leaders led their projects from scope development right through commissioning and startup. There are those in the projects world who firmly believe that an effective leader of a project in development will never be a good leader in execution and vice versa. The data clearly and forcefully disprove that belief.

WHAT IS THE ROLE OF THE ORGANIZATION?

What role does the organization have in creating an environment in which leadership can thrive? In general, companies and organizations that are careful about accountability, responsibility, and blame should produce a more hospitable environment for leaders to develop. One of the common characteristics of our successful project leaders is that they embrace accountability. They actively embrace a situation in which they and everyone concerned can see the relationship between how they perform and project outcomes. These leaders tend to be harder on themselves than the organization ever will be.

But there is a significant portion of companies with which we work in which every problem, no matter how small, needs a scapegoat. Such punitive cultures clearly make the risks associated with leadership much higher. What we find remarkable is that punitive cultures sometimes produce leaders anyway. At least three of our interviewed successful leaders work in organizations that either actively discourage risk-taking or punish failure without much search for cause. One of them works in an organization that is among the most punitive we have ever seen, actually firing project leaders outright who failed to meet sometimes hopeless expectations. Complex project leaders in punitive systems don't buck the system because to do so would result in isolation or dismissal. Instead, they work around the system by encouraging those who report to others to cooperate with them, by using network connections to circumvent problem people, and sometimes even "killing them with kindness." Even where the soil is not fertile, leadership can grow.

We do, however, see one type of organization that appears to produce true project leaders very infrequently or not at all: the process-driven, assurance-driven, consensus-decision-making-driven companies. These companies, of which there are quite a few, attempt to fix every problem with a new rule, a new procedure, or a new review process. As the vice-chairman of one of these companies once said to one of the authors, "Whenever anybody makes a mistake around here, we make a new rule that reads 'Don't be stupid anymore.'" These organizations produce no project leaders because they do not value people who stand out and who take a stand. The track record of these companies in complex projects is appropriately poor and probably cannot be improved without a rethinking of their culture.

In our experience, the best, most supportive cultures for project leadership development tend to respond calmly to project disappointments. When they have to intervene because an important project is going poorly, the focus is solely on recovery. The rest can be sorted out later. The managements in the best cultures tend to be very fact-driven. Yes, project failures must be understood because the biggest failure of all is to fail without learning. To quote one of our most successful complex project leaders, "On projects that we have had that didn't meet expectations, we were expected to (and allowed to) learn from those opportunities. This strengthened the next project. As our CEO told me after a project suffered problems, 'I can't fire you now, I have invested too much in your education!'" The supportive cultures *are always* driven from the top.[2]

SELECTING PROJECT LEADERS NOW

Picture yourself as a CEO, vice president, or agency leader with a critically important and difficult project coming up and you must select the project leader. You understand all that nice stuff we have been telling you about what you should have been doing to develop these people over the past 10 to 20 years, but that didn't happen and you live in the world of now, not in the world of what-if. How should you go about your task of selecting the right person? Below are the issues that we find to be central to your selection challenge.

Nature versus Nurture

One of the central unanswered questions implicit in this book is whether brilliant project leaders are born or made. This

---

[2] Another opportunity for corporate leadership is to facilitate better communication and coordination between Human Resources (HR) and the capital projects organization. HR often already has tools that could be used to generate better leader selection but rarely is involved in the process. Too often HR is not deeply familiar with the unusual requirements of the projects organization.

is, of course, a variation on an age-old question. Our study leads us to conclude that both nature and nurture are important. Personality (nature) appears to be necessary but not sufficient. More-closed personalities and those with less interest in people will probably never be good candidates for leading difficult projects. They will tend to find the most important tasks – articulating goals, aligning stakeholders, keeping everyone's spirits up, and communicating constantly – onerous tasks. And no matter how conscientious one might be, we humans tend to do less of the things that we find difficult and unrewarding.

So as a selector of a leader for your next important project, your first task has to be finding candidates with personalities and emotional intelligence makeups that form the basis of good project leadership. The same basics probably form the basis of good business leadership as well, so does it make sense to include good business leaders in the candidate pool? We have to say, probably not. First, we strongly suspect, although we cannot prove, that technical training and practice are necessary to provide credibility to the potential project leader. Second, and far more important, successful project leaders have a passion for capital projects. They find them challenging, exciting, and consistently interesting. Many complex project leaders describe each new project as an adventure. Joseph Brewer described leading the Sadara project in the Kingdom of Saudi Arabia as "like riding a rocket." Third, the candidate must be knowledgeable about project management. This does not mean, however, that only project managers are candidates. Those who have been very close to projects for much of their prior careers should be considered. Two of our interviewed successful leaders did not spend most of their early careers in project management. Joseph Brewer was an engineering leader before being selected to lead his first project and his selection was based on his leadership traits. Nora'in Salleh worked for a regulatory agency watching projects closely for her early career. Both Joseph and Nora'in were knowledgeable about project management without being project managers.

So how do you find project-knowledgeable people with what Tom Wolfe called the right stuff? Testing your pool of candidates with the Five-Factor Model and Emotional Intelligence Scale is probably a good first step.

The Right Experience

Although they tend to correlate, age is not experience. As we have discussed at several points in this book, many years of leading simpler projects may or may not have provided the candidate complex project leaders with useful background. It depends on what they did with it. Experience consists of the combination of the content of past situations and the capacity and facility of learning. The desired content are things such as:

- Broad and varied jobs
- Making timely decisions under conditions of uncertainty
- The opportunity to watch others lead complex projects
- Experience sorting out difficult interpersonal situations.

But experience without learning is just age. So, the critical question to ask the potential project leader is "How do you learn?" Those who have made the most of whatever experience has provided will be able to answer that question clearly and easily. They will provide a coherent model of how they assimilate and process their experiences into cumulative learning. They are very likely to tell you about pivotal moments in their development, and will almost certainly tell you about the people who have been most important in their journey. And this will cue you to another important bit of information: can your candidate tell stories?

Our experience is that every good leader is a good storyteller. The causality is clear. Humans are much better at remembering stories than any other form of information. It is baked into our DNA from tens of thousands of years without books. Leaders convey vision and goals through stories. Paul Harris's invention of the cathartic execution plan is a storytelling device. He is telling the future story of the new project. To test whether your candidate is a storyteller, sit down an hour after the interview and write down what you remember from the candidate's narrative. If it isn't a story, or if it is hard to recall much of anything from a list of facts, consider moving to the next candidate.

As you interview your leader candidates, ask yourself some simple questions: does this person make me feel at ease or wary? Do I connect with this person as a person, or only as a job-seeker? Am I more or less tense than I was 20 minutes ago when this interview started? The answers to these questions are important because the social skills underlying the answers are elements of what the candidate needs to lead a complex project.

What to Look for in a Decision-Making Approach

At a number of points in our study of project leaders, the issues of decision-making style and approach have come up. After all, the essence of good risk management is sound decision-making. Good decisions when problems arise, as they inevitably do in complex projects, are often the difference between success and failure. We are able to isolate a particularly successful leadership style: one that combines careful and genuine listening to all points of view and information available with a willingness to make timely and authoritative decisions, whether they are popular or not. We have also seen in other studies of these projects that effective leaders organize their projects so that most decisions are made by others, not by themselves.[3] Only those decisions with systemic implications are decided by the project leader.

Our successful project leaders were especially careful to avoid a decision-making style that diluted accountability. They were wary of peer reviews and too much assurance. They felt that time spent with steering committees was necessary but not value-adding. Successful project leaders also would really much rather select their own teams than leave personnel decisions to others. That is an important message for function-centered and weak-matrixed project organizations.

Implications for the Complex Projects of the Future

We would describe the past 15 years or so as a period of crisis and despair over the performance of complex projects. Numerous books have been written on the problematic performance of these projects and many have concluded that today's giant complex projects are simply unmanageable beasts and should be discontinued whenever possible.

After studying the leadership of these projects we come to quite a different conclusion and are much more optimistic. With the appropriate leadership, rather than management alone, these projects cannot only be done, they can be done well. To achieve success, however, the organizations that sponsor these projects must learn to select and, where needed, develop people who understand the leadership roles that these projects require. Our analysis demonstrates that this improved

---

[3] Edward Merrow, *Industrial Megaprojects* (Hoboken, NJ: Wiley, 2011), 185–198.

selection and development process is possible because the people who lead these projects well have clearly identifiable characteristics. Moreover, these characteristics can be measured, thereby eliminating much of the subjectivity and sometimes politics that have characterized the selection of project leaders in the past.

In no industrial sector is this improved selection and development process more important than in oil and gas. The reality of climate change notwithstanding, complex oil and gas projects will be necessary for a good while longer. The track record of these projects has been depressingly dismal. Failed petroleum development projects of the future will be ruinous to their sponsors because prices are very unlikely to bail bad projects out.

The other area that can clearly improve is large public infrastructure undertakings. These projects have often been problematic and their failures jeopardize the well-being of both developed and emerging economies. Better leadership is particularly important in these projects because the sponsors – governments and public/private partnerships – are often weak project organizations, which is to say they often lack basically sound project practices. Good leadership can mitigate many of these problems, although not completely eliminate them.

Complex projects are the building blocks of economies and societies. When they fail, we all fail and when they succeed, a better more prosperous world is created. The men and women who can lead these projects successfully are sorely needed. It is our hope that what we have learned in this journey can enable us to find and develop more of these remarkable people in the future.

INDEX